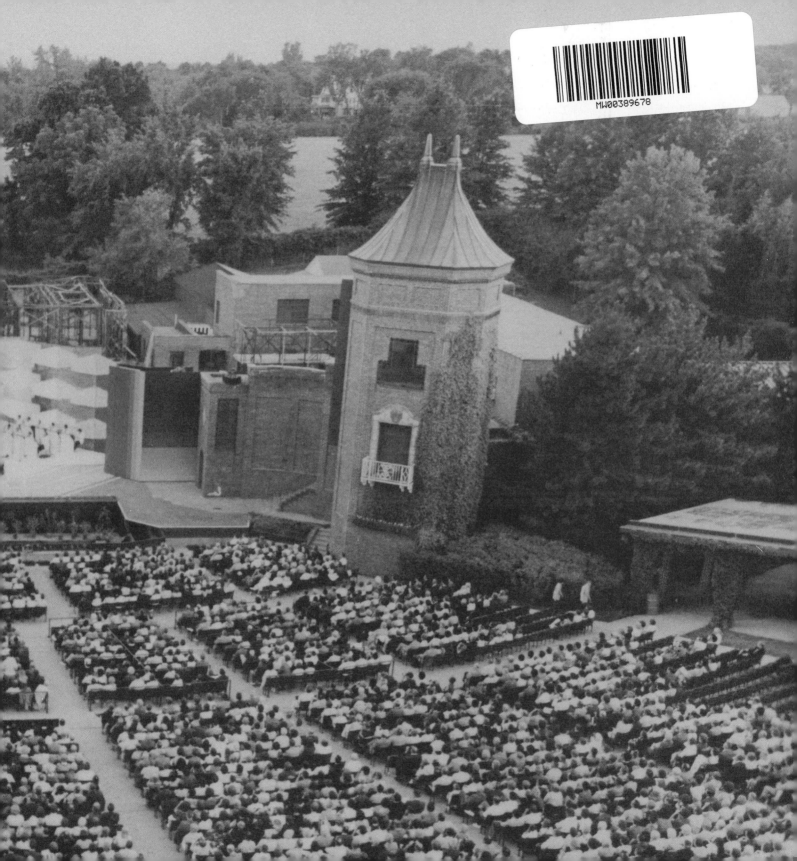

THE STORY OF

Starlight Theatre

THE STORY OF

Starlight Theatre

KATHLEEN HEGARTY THORNE

GENERATION ORGANIZATION
EUGENE, OREGON
1993

Book Design: Gwen Rhoads, Vesta Publishing Services
Front cover illustration: Jim Hamil
Editors: Jane Doyle Guthrie and Carol Gillette

Printed and distributed by:
The Lowell Press, Inc.
115 E. 31st Street
P. O. Box 411877
Kansas City, Missouri 64141

Published by:
Generation Organization
P.O. Box 5414
Eugene, Oregon 97405

To the fine people of Kansas City, thank you for the opportunity to spread happiness through the melodies of Starlight while adding joy to my own life.

I'm sure Kathy Thorne has found the same pleasure in writing this fine book. Read it— you'll love it!

Richard H. Berger

I was a forty-four-year-old graduate student when I decided to write about the
Starlight Theatre. I wanted to investigate the history of the place, the lay of the
land, the circumstances of the theatre's birth, and, most importantly, the people
who nurtured it and made it a success. Starlight is where I grew to love performing. I had danced and acted on its huge stage numerous times as a child,
and my adult concept of theatre was formed by that experience.

Kansas City is a part of me, and I am a small piece of its fabric. During the
late 1940s, before the age of television and air conditioning, my sister Twila and
I used to perform on the old Parks Department Band Wagon that traveled
throughout the city parks during the summer. Twila and I introduced "Kansas
City My Hometown" to summer audiences. The song was later adopted by the
City Council on March 27, 1950, as the official song of Kansas City. My mother
recently donated to the Kansas City Museum the original sheet music scripted
and notated by the composer, Joe Stern.

Since leaving the Midwest, I have performed, choreographed, and directed
musicals for high schools, community colleges, and community theatre groups.
When I was playing the role of Annie in *Annie Get Your Gun* in a small resort
town on the Oregon coast, the performance was held in a small gymnasium
that seated 300 at most. But when I stood on that stage with those temporarily
hung lights blinding me as to the size of my audience, I envisioned Starlight—
the vast expanse of seats that stretched almost as far as the eye could see. My
sense of character, her dynamics and power were determined by that vision.
Needless to say, I was loud.

The lessons, the heartaches, the fortunate choices of those who precede us
form a giant textbook for those who follow and who someday wish to lead. I
wanted the story of Starlight to be preserved. I wanted the story of Dick
Berger and Phil de Rosier and Bill Symon to be remembered. I wanted the
labors of Tony Ferrara, Ray Maier, Virginia Donovan, and Ancel Lacy to be
valued. I wanted the story to be available years hence to the young boy or girl now
sitting in an elementary school desk learning to read the words *dog* and *street* and
maybe someday *theatre*. I wanted this generation of Kansas Citians and the next to
know the story of their beautiful theatre. And so I wrote.

PHOTO COURTESY OF TWILA HEGARTY

**Author Kathleen Hegarty
Thorne** with Starlight's most
frequently seen leading man,
Donald Clarke. *Show Boat*, 1952.

ACKNOWLEDGMENTS

Thanks, Mom, for chauffeuring me around town all those years to dance school, to recitals, to park programs, and to Starlight.

Thanks to my father, a sports writer and Kansas editor of the *The Kansas City Star* for over thirty years, for inspiring me to put pen to paper, or, in this modern age, to put fingertip to computer key.

Thanks to my sister Twila for being my first dancing partner.

Thanks to Barbara Montgomery Kitchin for tending the fires so I could focus my attention on this book.

Thanks to Jeanne Roberts Landau of Kansas City and Nicole and Tim Foster of Eugene, Oregon for teaching me the love of dance.

Thanks to Sister Ancella Marie of Loretto Academy, Sister Felice of Avila College, and Horace Robinson and Dr. Grant McKernie of the University of Oregon for teaching me the love of theatre.

Thanks to John Doohan and Jim McQueeny, whose writings on the beginning of Starlight left a clear legacy.

Thanks to Janice Henderson Cohan, Paula Illmer West, Everett Thorne, Bill Lynch, and Dorothy Adkins for their help with editing.

Thanks to Jerry Funk and Aldon Ferrara, who spent many hours in interviews so that the Starlight story would be complete.

Thanks to *The Kansas City Star* library staff for their help in securing newspaper articles for reproduction in this book.

Thanks to Mary Beth and Robert Rohlf, who were most gracious with their time and who greatly facilitated the illustration of this book by loaning many of Starlight's photos to this project.

And very special thanks to Lew Thorne, my husband, my one and only Frank Butler of *Annie Get Your Gun*, without whose encouragement, patience, good humor, culinary, and computer skills this book would never have been written.

ACT FOUR

The Artists and Technicians

Set Designer – G. Philippe de Rosier *62*, Musical Director – Roland Fiore *66*,
Choreographer – Harding Dorn *70*, Stage Manager – Jerry Funk *73*,
Scenic Artist – Robert Benstead *75*, Master Carpenters – Ancel Lacy, Herman
Obermeyer, and Randy Halsey *75*, Prop Master – Al Krikorian *78*,
Costumes – Miss Audre and Virginia Donovan *80*, Soundman – Ray Maier *83*,
Lightmen – Burt Obermeyer and David Miller *86*.

ACT FIVE

Training Ground for Young Talent
93

Finale
103

The gentle rolling hills, eight miles south of where the Kansas and Missouri rivers meet, mark the spot where present day Starlight Theatre stands. Many native Americans transversed these hills throughout the centuries. Tribes of the Kansa, the Poncha, the Omaha and the Osage established their villages nearby. Even small groups of the Arapaho ventured this far east across the wide plains in search of food and adventure and witnessed the beauty of these hills.

In the 1820s government action in Washington, D.C., forced the migration of various eastern tribes to the newly established Indian lands west of the Missouri River. The Shawnee, Chippewah, Ottawa, Peoria, Miami, Seneca, and Cherokee all drew to the area. With this resettlement also came missionaries. And with the missionaries came other white men and women who eventually founded a town, built a city, and a century later constructed a huge amphitheatre on the hillside that would become nationally known in the mid-1900s for presentations of American musical theatre. The origin of that type of entertainment, however, began years before the founding of the town called Kansas City.

During the years 1828 through 1830, while Indians were being driven from the eastern woodlands to the open plains, a wandering entertainer named Thomas D. Rice traveled through Kentucky popularizing a form of entertainment known as minstrelsy. The first full-blown minstrel show featuring the Virginia Minstrels occurred in 1843. The group was headed by Daniel Emmett, the composer of "Dixie." Soon followed the Christy Minstrels, who entertained audiences with songs of Stephen Foster. The embryo of vaudeville was conceived in the olio medley acts that checkered these minstrel shows.

Much further to the east, across the Atlantic in Paris, a thirteen-year-old German boy procured an audition with the Director of the Conservatoire. Jacob Offenbach was accepted, unusual considering his age, but the youth did not stay for long. He soon struck out on his own. He began his performance career in a music shop, and his virtuosity on the cello brought his musical genius to the public's attention. In 1847 Offenbach wrote his first major work, a one-act comic opera called *L'Alcove*. This form of entertainment, known as operabouffe, was the precursor of the operetta. Twelve years later Offenbach wrote *Orpheus in the Underworld*, a work that established operetta as a genuine art form.

During this time on the northwestern Missouri plains, musical productions were far from the thoughts of the pioneers who struggled to build a home out of the wilderness.

American Musical and Kansas City History Time Line

	From time immemorable – The Land of the American Indian
1804	Lewis and Clark pass through
1806	Lewis and Clark return from the Pacific and scale the "Quality Hill" bluffs
1819	Jacob Offenbach is born in Cologne, Germany
1821	Beginnings of the first white man's settlement in Kansas City, Francois Chouteau warehouse
1825	Johann Strauss is born
1830	Forced migration of eastern Indian tribes to land just west of the Missouri border Missionaries soon follow
1832	The Mormons buy land in Jackson County to establish Zion
1834	Town of Westport established
1838	John Calvin McCoy, son of a missionary, builds outfitter's store (now Kelly's Bar) in Westport on the Oregon and Santa Fe trails
1843	First minstrel show opens in New York City in Chatham Square Theatre
1848	Discovery of gold in California sends thousands through Westport on route to gold fields
1850	McCoy and thirteen other men organize the township of Kansas
1854	*Kansas City Enterprise* newspaper is founded Robert Van Horn serves as editor whose goal is to secure Kansas City as the railroad crossroads to the West
1859	First full-scale operetta, *Orpheus in the Underworld* is presented
1864	First meeting of Offenbach and Strauss
1866	*The Black Crook*, the first musical to net over a million dollars, opens in New York
1867	Victor Herbert travels to Germany for intensive study
1869	Hannibal Bridge is completed connecting the eastern side of the Missouri River with "The West" Florenz Ziegfeld is born in Chicago Gilbert first meets Sullivan
1870	The Coates Opera House, first full-fledged theatre in Kansas City, opens
1874	*Die Fledermaus*, Strauss' masterpiece, appears
1875	Gilbert is officially introduced to Sullivan
1878	*H.M.S. Pinafore* takes New York by storm
1880	William Rockhill Nelson comes to Kansas City and establishes *The Kansas City Evening Star*

John Calvin McCoy, son of one of the early missionaries, formed a group of businessmen to buy a large flat shelf of rock at the Missouri River's edge, a natural wharf for supplies shipped up the Missouri River from St. Louis. The group purchased the 257 acres of prime farmland in order to form a township. They fussed over a name (for a time Possum Trot was a possibility), but finally settled on "Kansas," an Indian word meaning "smoky wind" or "people of the south wind." In 1850 the town of Kansas, population 700, was officially organized.

The great American civil upheaval did not leave Kansas City unscathed. Feeling on both sides of the slavery issue ran high in this area, located on the western end of a slave state and just across the river from a new territory with antislavery sentiments. Strife consumed the hills south of the little town as the blue and the gray armies crisscrossed them on their way to the bloody battle of Westport.

In the same year that Abraham Lincoln was reelected to the presidency, the two men most responsible for the popularity of operetta met in Europe at the Vienna Concordia-Ball, an event for which both had been invited to write waltzes. Jacob Offenbach met thirty-nine-year-old Johann Strauss and inquired, "Why haven't you written any operettas?"— a cutting remark meant to pique the younger composer of numerous musical works. Six years later Strauss did try his hand at operetta, and his first effort, *Indigo and the Forty Thieves*, opened in Vienna. Strauss eventually wrote eleven operettas, but his masterpiece, *Die Fledermaus*, did not appear until 1874.

In the latter part of the 1860s, Victor Herbert, one of the fathers of American operetta, resided with his mother and grandparents in a country house outside London. His aptitude for music was so apparent at an early age that his grandfather sent the young man and his mother to Germany for comprehensive musical training.

A musical production called *The Black Crook* opened in New York in 1866. Because of its scantily clad female dancers, ministers condemned the show and the public flocked to the performances. That first run at Niblo's Garden Theatre grossed one million dollars, a phenomenal sum at the time. *The Black Crook* sparked the interest of New York theatregoers as well as producers, who were quick to see that a musical presentation could be controversial, mediocre, but exceedingly profitable.

During the same year (1869) that the first railroad crossed over the Hannibal Bridge and cinched the destiny of Kansas City as the railroad crossing of America, Florenz Ziegfeld was born in Chicago. Gilbert also met Sullivan at the German Reed's Royal Gallery of Illustration in England (although their successful partnership was six years away).

Theatre ventures in Kansas City had begun before the Civil War. Stage performances had taken place in 1857 and 1858 in Frank's Hall and Long's Hall, both of which were on the second floors of buildings near Main and Fifth streets. The first full-fledged theatre was opened in 1870. The Coates Opera House, on the corner of Tenth and Broadway, offered a steady fare of dramas, music, and Italian and French operas until it burned in 1901. The Gillis Theater at Fifth and Main opened its doors in 1883 and bedazzled patrons with its ornate woodwork, frescoes, and draperies as well as its novel electric lighting. Warder Grand Opera House had its debut four years later.

In the year 1878 an English import washed ashore and created a sensation. Gilbert and Sullivan's *H.M.S. Pinafore* came to American audiences and provided material for parlor chatter for hundreds of New York theatre buffs. The American acceptance of English comic opera signaled the beginning of musical theatre as a serious contender for the public's entertainment dollar.

Two years after Gilbert and Sullivan's smash hit, newspaperman William Rockhill Nelson moved to Kansas City, established *The Kansas City Evening Star*, and began a private crusade to alter the destiny of his adopted town. *Evening Star* proclaimed the virtues of paved streets, better lighting, a more efficient police force, and aesthetically appealing surroundings for the city's inhabitants. Kansas City needed not only acres to expand but also expanded acres within the city limits, places for public recreation, playgrounds for children. It needed parks! Nelson enlisted the aid of other prominent citizens who would help promote his grand vision—S. B. Armour of the meat-packing industry, Kersey Coates, owner of the Opera House, Robert Gillham, Adriance Van Brunt, and August Meyer, the president of the parks program. Meyer was a wealthy industrialist who had made a fortune mining silver in Colorado and shipping it to his smelter in Kansas City's Argentine area. He was also a farsighted civic leader who shared Nelson's appreciation of a beautified city.

The Park Board, headed by Meyer, began wrestling with a physical growth plan for the young town. The board hired George Kessler as a city planner. Educated in Europe and an associate of Central Park designer Frederick Law Olmstead, Kessler believed

1883	Gillis Theater opens in Kansas City
1885	Jerome Kern is born
1887	Warder Grand Opera House opens in Kansas City
	Sigmund Romberg is born in Hungary
1888	Irving Berlin is born in Russia
1893	Cole Porter enters the world
1894	First revue, *The Passing Show*, appears
1895	Lorenz Hart and Oscar Hammerstein are born
1896	Thomas Swope donates park
1898	*Rice's Summer Nights*, first show ever written and performed by black entertainers, plays in a major Broadway house
1899	John Philip Sousa dedicates Kansas City's Convention Hall
	Scott Joplin writes "Maple Leaf Rag"
1902	Victor Herbert's *Babes in Toyland* and *The Wizard of Oz* open in New York
1904	George Balanchine is born in Russia
1905	Jule Styne is born in England
1906	George M. Cohan's "You're a Grand Old Flag" plays on the hit parade
1907	J. C. Nichols buys ten acres of land south of Kansas City. More than a decade later, he begins the development known as The Plaza
	First of Ziegfeld's *Follies*
1908	Sigmund Romberg immigrates to America
1911	Berlin's "Alexander's Ragtime Band" debuts
1912	Rudolf Friml replaces Herbert and composes *The Firefly*
1914	First of Jerome Kern's Princess Theatre shows, *The Girl from Utah,* is introduced
1916	First original score for a movie, *The Birth of a Nation*, is written by Victor Herbert
1918	Leonard Bernstein is born
1919	Actors Equity strike results in higher costs, smaller theatres, more intimate revues staged
1921	Dedication of the Liberty Memorial
	Shuffle Along, all negro revue, and Sigmund Romberg's *Blossom Time* open in New York
1924	New York offerings: George Gershwin's "Rhapsody in Blue"; Romberg's *The Student Prince*; Friml's *Rose Marie*
1926	*The Desert Song* by Sigmund Romberg opens in New York
	Queen Marie of Romania visits Kansas City
1927	Romberg's *The New Moon* opens out of town and closes due to poor reviews (later rewritten for the Broadway stage)
	Kern's and Hammerstein's *Show Boat* appears

that life in cities was unnatural, tending to stunt physical and moral growth. City dwellers were better and happier citizens if they had access to trees, open spaces, and unspoiled nature.

The hills and gullies, bluffs and creek beds that had caused so many headaches for early settlers offered quite an asset to this creative planner, who incorporated all these natural features within his designs. George Kessler, the designer of Hyde Park, Cliff Drive, Penn Valley Park, and the grounds of the present day Kansas City Art Institute, envisioned a system of boulevards that would connect all the city park areas and in turn be artful unto themselves. The funds necessary to begin such a project required voter approval, and not until 1895 did the park amendment pass.

A year later wealthy bachelor Thomas Swope donated 1,334 acres of land to the city. Located four miles south of town and thus considered "too far out" to be of any practical use to the citizenry, Swope Park nonetheless became part of Kansas City's park acreage. Meyer Boulevard, one of the many lovely avenues winding from the imagination of George Kessler, eventually led right to the entrance of this large park. Eleven years after Colonel Swope's gift, the Kansas City Zoological Society persuaded the Park Board to set aside sixty acres in Swope Park for the construction of a zoo. The face of the gentle hills that had seen the passing of centuries of Indian village life was soon to reflect young Kansas City's sense of recreation and desire for drama.

Two years preceding Swope's land gift, American musical theatre birthed the first of the revues, *The Passing Show*, in New York's Casino Theatre. While Cole Porter rocked and cooed in his mother's arms, young Jerome Kern pondered the complexities of playing a tune in the key of A flat, and Rudolf Friml entered the musical conservatory in his native Prague. Oscar Hammerstein II was then a two-year-old New Yorker living on 135th Street and struggling with an incredibly long name—Oscar Greeley Clendenning Hammerstein. (No wonder he went by the shortened version.)

At the turn of the twentieth century, Scott Joplin composed his "Maple Leaf Rag" in Sedalia, Missouri. Irving Berlin, who, in 1901, had left home at the age of thirteen to make his living singing in New York's Lower East Side saloons, was fascinated by Joplin's syncopated rhythms, so much so, that ten years later he composed "Alexander's Ragtime Band" and became known as the King of Ragtime. Two more musical babies were born—Meredith Willson, creator of *The Music Man*, in Iowa, and Richard Rogers in New York. In 1903 *The Wizard of Oz* made its debut, and Victor Herbert, the German immigrant who followed his soprano wife to America, presented "March of the Toys" to New York audiences as part of the *Babes in Toyland* score. A year later a woman was arrested for smoking a cigarette on New York's Fifth Avenue, and George Balanchine was born in St. Petersburg, Russia. Halfway through the first decade of the century, George M. Cohan's tunes "Mary's a Grand Old Name" (1905) and "You're a Grand Old Flag" (1906) captivated the public's ear.

John Philip Sousa dedicated Kansas City's Convention Hall in 1899, but it burned to the ground a year later. Not to be outwitted by chance, Kansas Citians reconstructed the hall in ninety days in time for the Democratic National Convention in July of 1900.

xvi

In 1907, while Ziegfeld was opening the first of his lavish *Follies*, Jerome Kern was making a lowly $12 a week as a songwriter in New York. A year later, the first radio station in America (later known as KQW in San Jose, California) went on the air, and "Shine on Harvest Moon" and "Take Me Out to the Ballgame" rose to the top of the national music charts. The year 1908 found Sigmund Romberg on a boat, crossing the Atlantic from his native Hungary and landing at Ellis Island. He secured a job in a pencil factory but soon was writing tunes for the Shubert productions.

When the war in Europe first began, the American continent remained relatively unaffected by the conflict. Jerome Kern penned the first of his Princess Theatre shows, *The Girl from Utah*, and the young Cole Porter transferred from the Harvard Law School to the School of Music. Two years later Victor Herbert wrote the first original score for a motion picture, *The Birth of a Nation*. The same year that America entered the war to make "the world safe for democracy," George Gershwin, an up-and-coming New York musician, was recommended as the rehearsal pianist for Kern's musical *Rock-a-Bye Baby*.

Following the war, Kansas City built and dedicated the Liberty Memorial. While jazz sounds were steaming from fifty or so clubs in the Twelfth Street area and political boss Tom Pendergast was puffing proudly on a cigar in his Nineteenth and Main office, musical compositions were flooding the New York stages. Rudolf Friml had received his first break in the American music world in 1912 when Victor Herbert became so disgusted with a certain temperamental lead soprano that he refused to write any more operettas for her. Friml took over the job and composed *The Firefly* with Otto Harbach. The mid-twenties then brought forth Friml's most successful operettas: *Rose Marie* (1924), *The Vagabond King* (1925), and *The Three Musketeers* (1928).

A year after George Gershwin wrote his 1924 *Rhapsody in Blue,* Richard Rogers gave up trying to write and sell songs, convinced that Tin Pan Alley and Broadway were not for him. He entered the business world—momentarily. Sigmund Romberg wrote lovely lasting music for his operetta *The Desert Song,* which played in New York for 465 performances (and eventually at Kansas City's Starlight Theatre for the first seven nights of its existence).

Jerome Kern and Oscar Hammerstein II joined forces to produce a show business bonanza that marked the "birth of the American book musical." Edna Ferber's fiction provided the story, and Flo Ziegfeld placed the production in his own extravagant theatre. The show that resulted clearly demonstrated that American audiences would accept and support a musical endeavor that was not filled with comic elements, glitzy dances, snappy tunes, and happy endings. The production: *Show Boat*, 1927.

During those years of the 1920s when New Yorkers feasted on the musical experimentation going on around them, Kansas Citians busied themselves looking for the means and the place to build an outdoor theatre for concerts and musical plays. The timeless rolling hills, backdrop and stage to years of migration and war, offered the perfect spot. The civic interest that eventually built Starlight Theatre arose within the same time period that the American musical, as we know it, was born.

The Beginnings of Starlight

S TARLIGHT IS A MAGIC PLACE. An evening at the Swope Park theatre stands apart from any other event. You sit under the stars, sometimes under the rain clouds, feel the cool breeze, listen to the cicadas chirp and the seals bark in the nearby zoo, and watch the thousands assemble. As the last of daylight slips into the western horizon, a spotlight beams on the conductor, the noise of the crowd fades to a hush, and the strains of America's best melodies fill the summer air. The stage lights come up, the score swells, the script begins to breathe, and the artistic process begins, punctuated by a firefly overhead, or by the faint sounds of a city not yet finished with the day's chores.

Unlike many other art forms, live theatre is a participatory experience, an event that the spectator helps to create. Rather than looking at a canvas already bespeckled with paint, or a piece of celluloid already imprinted, theatregoers witness the process of creation. And there's an edge to that creative process, the possibility of human error. Perhaps the actor will forget, perhaps the chair will crack, or perhaps the next dance will be all the more lively because the dancer can feel your energy and sense your approval. You view the action from your seat, yet your mind and sometimes your heart leap on stage with the actor, the dancer, or the singer who expresses your own longing to touch the core of life or simply to laugh at life's ridiculous moments.

Every audience is unique because every set of circumstances that come together for a performance is different. Yet the experience of an evening in Kansas City's hillside ampitheatre links millions of Midwesterners who have gone to the theatre in Swope Park and come away refreshed, insightful, and, often, amused.

Starlight has become nationally known for its presentation of musical theatre. Light opera, operettas, and book musicals have enchanted audiences there for over four decades. The spoken word, enriched with moving melodies and accentuated by dance, conveys an absorbing message. When powerfully presented, the message speaks so strongly of the truth that the experience takes hold of the heart and doesn't

Left: **Opening Night** at Starlight, *The Desert Song*, June 25, 1951.

THE DESERT SONG • RIO RITA • SONG OF NORWAY • ROBERTA • ROSE MARIE • THE CHOCOLATE SOLDIER • BRIGADOON • BITTERSWEET • BABES IN TOYLAND • NAUGHTY MARIETTA • THE GREAT WALTZ • GOOD NEWS • THE VAGABOND KING • WHERE'S CHARLEY? • THE FIREFLY • CAROUSEL • ROBIN HOOD • EAST WIND • THE RED MILL • SHOW BOAT • THE STUDENT PRINCE • THE WIZARD OF OZ • THE MERRY WIDOW • BLOOMER GIRL • ON YOUR TOES • UP IN CENTRAL PARK • THE NEW MOON • KISS ME KATE • BLOSSOM TIME • ANNIE GET YOUR GUN •

let go. Since 1951 Starlight Theatre has spotlighted those musical moments. This theatre in Swope Park has been and continues to be a showplace for the very best that the American musical theatre has to offer.

QUEEN OF ROMANIA VISIT

Queen Marie of Romania.
Circa 1920.

The idea of a theatre "under the stars" began circulating in Kansas City during the early 1920s. Many citizens were interested in building a performance area, but credit for initiation of funds goes to The Kansas City Federation of Music Clubs. The 1926 visit of Queen Marie of Romania proved the impetus for launching the project. The Standard Oil Company organized a cross-country tour as a goodwill gesture for the queen and her two children, Prince Nicholas and Princess Illeana. Her country had just recently made its oil fields available, and a happy queen would be a political and economic asset to the American oil company. As a six-hour stopover was scheduled for Kansas City, the music club saw a prime opportunity to showcase local talent. The group planned a public reception and simple ceremony at the Liberty Memorial for the early evening, followed by a musical presentation in the American Royal building.

Five years earlier, Vice President Calvin Coolidge and the Allied commanders of World War I—General John Pershing, General Marshal Foch of France, Admiral Lord Beatty of Great Britain, Lieutenant General Baron Jacques of Belgium, and General Armando Diaz of Italy—had gathered in Kansas City for the dedication of the site of the Liberty Memorial; happily for the organizers of Queen Marie's reception, however, the official dedication of the site was scheduled on the very same day as her arrival in November of 1926. President Calvin Coolidge addressed a huge crowd assembled for the honors, but after he stepped on the train headed for the East, many of the dignitaries in their silk hats and cutaways, and a throng of the townspeople dressed in their finery, simply swept from one momentous ceremony to another.

This author's aunt, Dorothy Bennett Adkins, was carried on her father's shoulders in order to glimpse the monarch and her children as they arrived on the Chicago, Burlington & Quincy railroad from Nebraska. The crowd grew so huge that the queen herself described it as colossal. During the musical section of the festivities, those who sat near the royalty in the specially constructed box seats paid $100 for the honor of doing so. Prices for arena floor seats were $2.50. In all, the occasion realized a $7,000 profit. The funds were placed in the city trust to be used for some sort of outdoor stage or band shell in one of the city parks.

A German Opera Company

In the spring of 1930, the Chamber of Commerce attempted to interest the Chicago Opera Company in a series of performances in Kansas City, but a compatible schedule could not be worked out. At the suggestion of Walter Fritschy, the concert man, the Chamber next approached the German Grand Opera Company. The four operas comprising *The Ring of the Nibelungs* cycle were brought to Kansas City. William Symon, the manager of the Convention Bureau for the Kansas City, Missouri, Chamber of Commerce, raised $36,000 among 225 guarantors as an underwriting fund. The week's performances proved such a social and artistic success that a return engagement of the opera company was proposed; however, some of the businessmen frankly admitted that one week of Wagner's works was quite enough. Perhaps a season of light opera could be substituted? In the end, booking arrangements for other light opera companies could not be made, and the organizers dropped their idea of yearly operatic offerings. The German Opera performances, however, did help spark the drive for an outdoor theatre. The 55,000 attendance figure showed that Kansas Citians would support such a venture, and Symon's guarantor system proved the feasibility of gathering adequate financial backing. Symon would utilize that same system of guarantors years later after becoming the first business manager for Starlight Theatre.

John A. Moore was an early proponent of the theatre. He became the first Starlight Association president.

False Construction Starts

In 1932 a construction start was made on the grounds of the old August Meyer home, or, as it is known today, the Kansas City Art Institute. Not many nails had been pounded before neighbors began to complain about the nuisance possibilities of so large a structure in a residential neighborhood. The city zoning board agreed, and the plans for an outdoor theatre were shelved.

Proponents next considered erecting a temporary stage just north of the University of Kansas City (present day University of Missouri at Kansas City) in 1934; however, the projected cost of $10,000 seemed high, and questions arose as to whether the newly completed Municipal Auditorium would prove too much competition. Once again plans for an outdoor theatre faded into the blueprint.

Six years later the Park Board commissioned A. W. Archer to design a performance shell, and he came up with a model of one he proposed for Swope Park. This "Music Temple," envisioned just northwest of the band pavilion, would have seated 5,700 to be increased to 11,000 and encompassed a stage able to accommodate a 100-piece band. John A. Moore, then president of the Park Board, along with Edwin Chandler and H. H. Peters, board members, J. V. Lewis, superintendent of

parks, and John Lacy, secretary, traveled to St. Louis to talk with officials at the St. Louis Municipal Opera about the pros and cons of a shell. They learned that a shell was too limiting; though quite acceptable for musical concerts, such a structure would prove too restrictive for musical play presentations.

CITIZENS' PLANNING COUNCIL AND THE CENTENNIAL ASSOCIATION

John Moore remained very interested in an outdoor theatre for Kansas City, and following his term on the Park Board he was named chairman of the outdoor theatre committee of the Citizens' Planning Council. He initiated a four-year comprehensive study by the board and executive staff. The board commissioned a prominent Kansas City architect to make a study of existing outdoor theatres and to come up with a design suitable to the city's needs. The board hired Edward Buehler Delk.

Born in Schoharie, New York, in 1885, Delk had graduated from the University of Pennsylvania with a B.S. degree and traveled through Greece and Italy for four months with Lorado Taft, sketching many Greek and Roman temples and public buildings. After fulfilling his military obligations as an Air Force first lieutenant in World

Left to right: **J. V. Lewis,** Superintendent of Parks; Edward B. Delk, architect of Starlight Theatre; John Lacy, secretary of the Park Board; Holland Wheeler, Assistant Superintendent of Parks.

The tennis courts under which Starlight Theatre was built. *Photo courtesy of James Shoemaker, Park Planner for the city of Kansas City, Missouri.*

PHOTOS COURTESY OF STARLIGHT THEATRE

War I, he enrolled in graduate studies at the University of London to further his already extensive knowledge of architecture. He was a proven architect in Philadelphia before moving to Kansas City in 1920.

Delk worked for the Kansas City architectural firm of Hare and Hare. Among his many accomplishments were the designs of St. Andrew's Church at Wornall Road and Meyer Boulevard, the D. W. Newcomer's Funeral Home on Brush Creek Boulevard, and the Schuyler Ashley Hall at Pembroke Country Day School. Further, his adaptation of Frank Lloyd Wright's Community Christian Church at Forty-sixth and Main streets brought the design within the city's building code requirements. Delk also consulted for the J. C. Nichols Investment Company, and was largely responsible for the grand design of the Country Club Plaza.

Edward Delk was an experienced architect, but not an experienced theatrical one. To augment his own understanding of the special needs of a theatre, especially an outdoor facility with seating for 7,854, he visited many existing outdoor theatres all over

Above and left: **Views** of the audience area from the stage during construction.

The pylons being erected.

the world and catalogued numerous ideas and bits of information relevant to performance structures. For example, he discovered that brick construction was preferable to stone; stone reflected light so that the light could not be concentrated on the stage.

Through the efforts of the Citizens' Planning Council and the members of the Park Board, the outdoor theatre proposal became part of the city's post-war bond issue of 1947, but only after $250,000 had been subtracted from the plan. The voters approved the first $500,000 toward construction of the theatre itself. To this was added another $225,000 for the parking lot, roadways, and other improvements. The construction of an outdoor theatre, though, fell very low on the city's list of priorities.

What activated a sense of immediacy were the upcoming ceremonies accompanying Kansas City's 100th birthday. The Centennial Association, headed by Herbert H. Wilson, had to find a site for a pageant depicting the events in the city's early history. Carter Tucker, then the head of the Park Board, suggested Swope Park for the attraction. Although the bond money earmarked for the theatre was in litigation, a resourceful and hard-working centennial group contributed $135,000 to begin construction.

The precise location chosen for the theatre in Swope Park lay beneath the existing tennis courts. Bulldozers were readied and construction began on a cold December day in 1949. Planners moved the theatre site some twenty-five feet north in order to preserve several majestic trees that provided a beautiful backdrop. Within two weeks more than six hundred trees were removed from the site. Workmen labored in subzero weather to extract ten thousand yards of solid rock from the present-day box seat section. It was not uncommon to see 150 craftsmen at a time working steadily against the clock to ready the theatre for its June debut. Jim McQueeny, Starlight's first publicity director, recorded the early construction data: Concrete totaling one thousand six hundred cubic yards and twenty-two tons of steel went into the auditorium area on schedule despite a truck drivers' strike and one at a sand plant. Cement finishers toiled until midnight night after night completing ramps and sections of the slab so that the seats could be installed at the rate of four hundred per day. Grading operations began in January, and, by late spring, sewers, the underground electrical system, and reinforced concrete slabs for seats, the roadways, and parking areas were all well

THE STORY OF STARLIGHT THEATRE

on the way to completion.   However, a rail strike prevented the delivery of seat bottoms, so metal chairs were rented and secured to the standards of the permanent seats.

"THRILLS OF THE CENTURY" PAGEANT

The historical revue "Thrills of the Century" opened at Starlight Theatre on June 4, 1950, and continued through July 10.   Hundreds of local townspeople participated in the event.   (See "Thrills" program pages 129–132.)   The extravaganza began with a greeting from the pageant's royal court, complete with the queen's crowning on opening night by movieland's Gloria Swanson.   When queen Clara Belle Smith and her court exited the stage, the lights dimmed and out of the darkness came the low moan of a single airplane engine.   Another engine joined in and then another, until a mighty crescendo of sound became the background for the opening words of the pageant: "Hear that! There is the song of progress, of a modern age, of speed and power, of faith and courage.   A song symbolizing a city, a great city with a hundred years of achievement."

From the opening scenes of airplanes, bands of Indians, and covered wagons, the pageant progressed through events in the city's history: the visit of "The Princess of the Missouri" to the court of Louis XV, the coming of the steamboat of Major Stephen Long, a Jesuit missionary's visit to Chouteau's settlement, and a speech attributed to Senator Thomas Hart Benton.   Thunderous gunfire and a sky illuminated by fireworks provided atmosphere for "The Battle of Westport."   The star of the pageant was the original locomotive that had crossed the Hannibal Bridge eighty-one years before, chugging out on stage on specially built rails.   One of the most memorable moments occurred when a team of oxen hitched to a six-hundred-pound cart broke loose, thundering across the stage, scattering hundreds of actors, and crashing into new cars on loan to the pageant by a local automobile dealer. A Gay '90s revue was

The Beginnings of Starlight

Article reproduced by permission of *The Kansas City Star.*

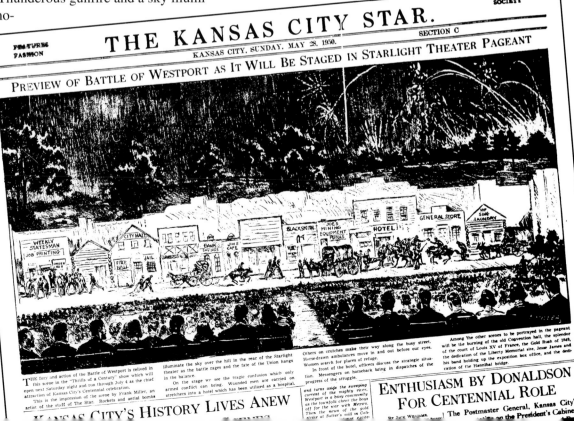

followed by fire bells, which rang en route to extinguishing the flames of old Convention Hall. Pearl Harbor Day was marked with simplicity and realism; two families sat on stage, hearing the news of the Japanese attack, and in unison their men rose to go and serve the country. The pageant ended with fireworks, flags, and groups of men and women representing each of the armed services lined up before a backdrop of the Kansas City skyline.

John Doohan, reporter for *The Kansas City Star*, wrote that thousands flocked to the park to witness this spectacular city saga. The attendance figure for just the Fourth of July performance neared eight thousand. The pageant's appeal prompted the Park Board to move ahead with plans to complete the theatre. In July of 1950, the City Council appropriated $213,000 for more improvements. A later Park Board request for $160,000 was also granted in January of 1951.

THE STARLIGHT THEATRE ASSOCIATION

Citizens' dollars built Starlight Theatre, and it rightfully belonged to the public. But who would be responsible for this facility? Who would guide its decisions, pay for its mistakes, and hire the personnel necessary to produce top quality musical performances? The answer to all these questions rested in the establishment of the Starlight Theatre Association. A mailing went out to a group of Kansas Citians inviting them to become charter members of the Association. A total of 586 persons sent in their checks for $10. The Starlight Association was and remains today a group of citizens who give of their time to oversee the policies and management of the theatre.

The Association is a non-profit group that, according to its bylaws, cannot distribute any funds to its members, purchase land, or use funds to influence legislation or to support any political campaign. For the first three decades, the president, five or more vice presidents, a secretary, and a treasurer were elected annually, and their term of office could not exceed three successive years. In 1981 a reorganization took place paring down the number of active Association members to thirty. Today there is a president, a treasurer, three vice presidents, a secretary, and the general manager on the board.

Newly constructed Starlight Theatre.

PHOTO COURTESY OF STARLIGHT THEATRE

THE STORY OF STARLIGHT THEATRE

Twenty-three other individuals comprise the rest of the membership. The Association rents the Starlight facility from the Park Board for $1 a year.

The 1951 election of officers ushered in John A. Moore as the first president. (See the Starlight Association Presidents listing p. 127.) A partial list of the board of directors was drawn up, and plans were made for raising $200,000 to activate the theatre. Of this sum, $100,000 was to be in cash, with the remaining funds to be held on call in the event of a deficit. L. Russell Kelce was chosen to head the finance committee, with William Symon as vice chairman and J. Guy Robertson as the executive secretary of the fundraising activity. These men began organizing the same guarantor system Symon had used twenty-one years before in securing the German Opera Company's performances.

Civic pride worked overtime during those early months of 1951. Professionals from the community volunteered their time to form committees that would establish theatre policy, while craftsmen labored double shifts in order to ready the facility itself. Citizens contributed dollars and talents in order to secure a steady and sound future for this infant theatre that many Kansas Citians had worked for a quarter of a century to bring into existence.

PHOTO COURTESY OF STARLIGHT THEATRE

The theatre is completed and ready for the opening season of 1951. Note the early plantings of trees.

The Beginnings of Starlight

9

A Unique Production Facility

STARLIGHT THEATRE and its support buildings occupy more than fourteen acres of park area. The theatre itself looks much like the facility that Edward Delk originally designed. Despite his inexperience in theatre architecture, Delk developed basic plans that proved highly functional for an outdoor entertainment area. Having studied the layout of many existing outdoor theatres, he realized the importance of finding a perfect location, one where the patrons could see and hear the action on stage despite the immense distance from the performers. When Swope Park was suggested as the site for Starlight, Delk's architectural plans took form. The stage area, the audience area (with its nearly perfect slope), the giant light pylons on each side of the stage, and the light bridge across the back of the seating area were all in place on opening night, June 25, 1951. The original cost of the facility was $1,750,000; estimates of its present-day value range upward of $40,000,000!

Starlight was patterned after the St. Louis Municipal Opera, known as the Muny. Frank Mayfield, an official of the Muny, and Paul Beisman, its manager, offered inestimable help in counseling with the Kansas City planners.

STAGE

The Muny Opera is the only outdoor theatre in the country that has a larger seating capacity than Starlight, but the Kansas City facility presents the bigger stage. In fact, Starlight has the largest outdoor stage in the country. In its initial configuration, it was also farther away from the audience than any other. The front of the present stage measures just over 284 feet from the base of the lighting towers at the rear, quite close to the length of a football field!

Delk's plans called for a revolving stage at Starlight. A pit was built during original construction so that one could be fashioned at a later date, the cost in 1951 being

Left: **Starlight audience area** as seen from the west pylon.

CALL ME MADAM • SWEETHEARTS • THE THREE MUSKETEERS • GIRL CRAZY • CARMEN • GENTLEMEN PREFER BLONDES • HIT THE DECK • NO NO NANETTE • OKLAHOMA! • ME AND JULIET • GUYS AND DOLLS • FINIAN'S RAINBOW • COLE PORTER FESTIVAL • WONDERFUL TOWN • SOUTH PACIFIC • PETER PAN • KISMET • BEST FOOT FORWARD • PLAIN AND FANCY • PAINT YOUR WAGON • WISH YOU WERE HERE • THE KING AND I • HIGH BUTTON SHOES • CAN CAN • BY THE BEAUTIFUL SEA • THE PAJAMA GAME • PANAMA HATTIE • SILK STOCKINGS •

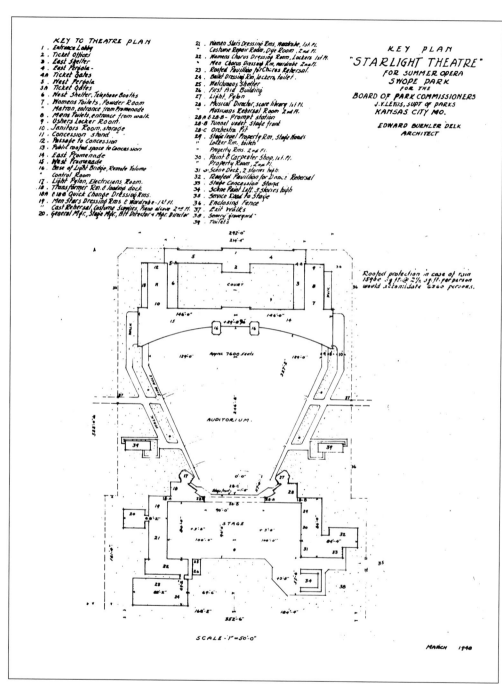

Roofed protection in case of rain
15960 sq ft @ 2½ sq ft per person
would accommodate 6360 persons.

SCALE 1" = 50'-0"

MARCH 1940

Delk's key plan for Starlight Theatre.

too prohibitive. But when workers installed the permanent stage in 1954, planners virtually abandoned the idea of a stage that would revolve. During the first three years of operation, the stage was left open to the weather and the flooring deteriorated so badly that it needed replacing each year. The 1954 stage designed by Holland Wheeler, assistant superintendent of parks, was built in sixteen sections to allow for removal and storage at the end of each season. The entire thirty-five-foot depth of the acting area was covered with two-by-six-inch maple boards. The boards of the St. Louis Muny stage stood on edge, but the maple flooring for Starlight's stage laid flat. Craftsmen installed the planks an eighth of an inch apart to permit rainwater to flow into the drains beneath. This giant stage came out of storage each spring, to be reassembled, sanded, and repainted for the new season.

The stage lasted thirty-three years. Toward the end of that time, the boards began to crack, causing concern for actors and especially for dancers. In 1987 the old maple was torn out and replaced with 3/4 inch plywood (maple flooring was no longer available or affordable). The bottom layer of the wooden stage is CCA treated plywood but with a rough finish. A new smooth top layer of plywood is bolted in place every year. The 1987 stage also added four new sections to the front part of the stage, moving the playing area nine feet closer to the audience which translates to every seat being four rows closer to the performers. The back four sections of the

stage are concrete in order to support the weight of the huge rolling scene wagons. The stage does not slant down to the audience area because the scenery wagons will not roll on a slanted surface.

The pit being dug for the revolving stage, 1950.

SCENERY WAGONS

Starlight's large scenery wagons are unusual among theatres. Measuring ten by thirty-six feet long and eighteen feet high, they are mounted on huge casters. The original scene wagons were designed and built by Ancel Lacy, Starlight's first master carpenter, and his crew. Twenty-two new scenic units built in the spring of 1977 completely replaced all the originals. The wagons require a crew of men to roll them into position. In order to steady the units, the men wrap chains around the casters and tie down the scene wagons with huge ropes. The men thread these ropes through large

A Unique Production Facility   13

rings cemented into the backstage concrete. The need for secure anchors has been demonstrated more than once when the large muslin flats have caught the hefty gusts of Kansas City summer winds and begun floating across the stage.

Stage carpenters build scenery for the wagons on a scale of 18':8'. That means that the average room height of eight feet is made eighteen feet high for Starlight audiences. Much bigger than life, such a scale lends itself to spectacle. G. Philippe de Rosier, Starlight's resident set designer for twenty-four years, described the challenge in an interview with William Foster of *The Independence Examiner*: "The size and layout of the Starlight Theatre compels us to upstage our productions—be 'theatrical' if you will. We have to overscale and distort our sets. If we didn't, the scenes would look too small and the actors would appear to be giants."

Above: **Scenery wagons** being rolled into position.

Below: **Flats** being prepared in backstage area.

FLATS

Starlight sets require special treatment of the muslin flats and the paint put on them because of exposure to the open air. With the perils of moisture and extreme heat, without proper precautions the muslin can stretch or contract, and the paint can run off the canvas. Randy Halsey, the present master carpenter for Starlight Theatre, explains:

The scenery for each show represents a large complicated puzzle. The puzzle is comprised of 200 to 300 individual pieces (flats), which are wooden frames of varying sizes and configurations. Each flat is covered with muslin that has been glued in place using organic animal-based adhesive called

THE STORY OF STARLIGHT THEATRE

casein. Casein is used because it is non-water soluble, important because it will not neutralize in the first summer rainstorm, yet can be manually separated and reglued. Each flat must be prepared with whiting solution, which is brushed on the muslin to shrink it, add body, and provide a clean surface for painting. Until 1987 casein-based pigments were used as the artist's medium. The supersaturated colors allowed for great flexibility and creativity in tone quality and use of application, however remained water soluble. To seal them from the elements, laboratory formaldehyde was applied to the finished product. Today, latex paints, with their own intrinsic binder, and acrylic sealers are used.

In an ordinary theatre that has curtains on the top and sides of the stage area, hiding the edges of scenery presents no problem; the open Starlight stage that has no proscenium, however, creates extra perplexities for the scenic people who must adapt and improvise the design of the scenery to create a finished image for the audience.

Scene from *Kiss Me Kate* (1953) in front of the act curtain.

ACT CURTAIN

When Starlight first opened, much discussion ensued about an act curtain. A front curtain for an outdoor theatre had never been constructed—anywhere. Broadway production experts came to Kansas City in 1951 to talk with Richard Berger, the first director-producer. Berger brought in Starlight's master carpenter, Ancel Lacy, for the meeting. Technical terms and dire predictions filled the room. The curtain couldn't be constructed, so said the "Broadway experts." Lacy, a carpenter not trained in school but a highly schooled craftsman, stayed more quiet than usual. He sat to the side, listened, asked a few questions, and took a few notes with his stub pencil. That was all. A month or so before the opening performance, Lacy had completed the preliminary work. The talented

A Unique Production Facility

Above: **The act curtain** parted for scene from *Rose Marie* (1951).

master carpenter had designed the huge curtain for the seventy-foot-wide stage area so that it would open and close in a matter of eighteen seconds. At Lacy's suggestion it was louvered to minimize the possibility of destruction by wind. The curtain had two sections, each of which rolled out from opposite sides of the stage. The sections joined and parted simultaneously, moving on rollers and guided by rails. There was no other curtain like it in the world.

The act curtain, as well as the huge scene wagons, were built by Ancel Lacy, John Hogan, Herb Obermeyer, James Craig, Ed Maier, Walter Brown, H. G. "Spike" Milligan, and Harold Elliott at Shelter House #1 (the stage could not be used as a building area because it was not yet completed). At first the huge scene wagons were rolled down from the shelter house, but by the time they arrived at the stage area, the casters were "the size of marbles" and the crew that had worked all day pushing them was exhausted. The rest of the wagons and the act curtain were later trucked down to the theatre and put into place. In 1983, with the advent of the light canopy over the Starlight stage, the act curtain designed by Ancel Lacy was retired from service.

PERGOLAS

By 1953 a most urgently needed addition to the theatre, as far as the patrons were concerned, was some sort of shelter from rain. Alarms were sounded. All sorts of suggestions were made, ranging from canvas strips supported by metal poles to permanent pergolas. The general definition of a pergola depicts an arbor, usually with an open roof of cross rafters or latticework. What Starlight patrons had in mind, though, was not an open-roofed structure! Shelter, dry clothes, a safe haven in a storm—these were the sentiments that prompted the cry for covered areas. Planners approached

Edward Delk with suggestions for covered walkways. Delk responded with roofed pergolas in keeping with the style and flavor of the original brick architecture. He situated the pergolas on each side of the audience area, each being two hundred twenty-five feet long and twenty-seven feet wide. Precast concrete slabs, each weighing four tons, formed the base for the roofs. J. V. Lewis, superintendent of parks, announced in April of 1954 that the structures would be completed for the summer season. They were.

Again money was an issue. City officials accommodated the planners by agreeing to pay the entire cost of $50,781 and then allow Starlight to repay the amount over a period of years.

SUPPORT BUILDINGS

Backstage additions were made as they became necessary. The pavilions, costume shop, offices, dressing rooms, and cafeteria facilities were all constructed by 1951. Ancel Lacy supervised the building of the carpentry shop in 1952. The following year Lacy and his crew added a corrugated metal scene shop. Several years later another metal building joined the stage right area to provide storage for flats and props. The muslin flat frames are saved and reused each year as are unusual props and scenic elements. These are stored in the stage right buildings. In the early 1960s a new and

The pergolas as shown from the audience area.

PHOTO COURTESY OF LEW THORNE

permanent ticket office was constructed adjacent to the front gates of the theatre. Delk's original design had included the ticket office as part of the overall structure, but lack of funds delayed its arrival on the Starlight grounds for twelve years.

SEATING AREA

Because Starlight is an outdoor facility exposed to a wide variety of weather conditions, equipment aging and disrepair is a common problem. The old wooden seats required constant checking and repair after each winter and even during the summer months after severe winds or hailstorms. In addition, every morning during the season, the seats were hosed down for the night's performance. In 1982 and 1983, as part of a five-year theatre improvement plan, sturdy plastic seats replaced all the old wooden ones at a cost of $780,000.

The arrangement of the seating area for 7,854 has remained the same since 1951. The price of the tickets has not. In 1952 there were still more than fifty-four hundred seats nightly in the 50 cents to $1.50 range. By 1961 the orchestra seats were selling for $3.50, the loges for $3.00, box seats for $4.00, the middle section of the audience area for $2.00 and $2.50, and the back section for $1.00 and $1.50. Fourteen years later the prices had risen to $6.50 and $7.00 for orchestra and box seats, $4.00 to $6.00 for the middle section, and $1.50 to $2.40 for the rear section. The prices for the late '80s season listed $56 for orchestra and box seats, $40 for the middle section, and $24 for the rear section. By 1992, though, the price for an orchestra seat had dropped to $27, with comparable reductions for all other sections.

Top: **Delk's rendition** of the proposed ticket office. The ticket office actually constructed in 1963 lacks the ornate features.

Bottom: **The paint shop.**

THE STORY OF STARLIGHT THEATRE

RAIN CHECK POLICY

In the 1950s and 1960s, the official curtain time was 8:15 p.m. During the 1970s, starting time was changed to 8:30 p.m. Throughout all these years, Starlight has maintained the same rain check policy for over forty years: in case of rain, the beginning of the show may be delayed up to one hour. If rain continues past that point, the production is canceled and rain checks are issued for subsequent performances. If all other performances of that show have been sold out, the patron is entitled to a refund or a seat for another show.

Every Starlight program contains the following sentence: "the term 'one hour's performance' does not mean a continuous hour." This statement offers the key to understanding the procedure for refunds and substitutions. Rain can interrupt the show several times during an evening, but if the production has had at least one hour of playing time, not necessarily continuous playing time, the show is canceled and no refund or ticket substitution is given. For this reason, many performers on stage and musicians in the pit have continued on with the show while drenched to the bone. The audience can seek shelter under umbrellas, raincoats, or the pergolas; the players, however, must persevere for sixty minutes in order to fulfill the theatre's obligation to its customers.

Rain has caused other types of headaches for the management. For example, in 1961 the opening night of *Flower Drum Song* was devoid of an audience. A deluge had driven off everyone, everyone except Dick Berger, who was the producer, the cast, and, on Berger's insistence, the local critic. Berger reasoned that the performances for subsequent nights would be ill attended if the usual Tuesday review did not appear in the local newspaper. So he contrived to have the entire show performed on the singers' pavilion. Susan Kingwill, the present musical conductor at Starlight, was the musician who stayed late that night to provide the piano accompaniment. The stars and the ensemble performed the entire play for the two member audience and Berger got his review the next day.

Ethel Merman in rehearsal for *Call Me Madam,* 1968.

REHEARSAL SCHEDULE

Organization of rehearsal time is mandatory. Actors Equity, the stage performers' union, has very specific rules regarding how many hours per week its members can be expected to work, under what conditions, and for what salary. In the early 1950s and 1960s, the union governed the stage directors, the choreographer, and the actors, singers, and dancers. Because Starlight cannot give a matinee, the union allowed the theatre to work its members seven days and seven nights a week. Two half-days were written into the schedule as time off for actors and ensemble members. During the late '50s the chorus members worked eighty hours a week for $75. The rehearsal schedule looked something like this:

Monday through Wednesday, principal characters blocked their stage movements and walked through their lines, often in the space behind the back section of the audience area. The width of the area was similar to that of the stage, but was covered and thus offered protection from the intense heat. The choreographer had the dancers on the backstage east pavilion learning the dance routines for the upcoming show. The assistant music director kept the singers on the west pavilion rehearsing the songs. The conductor, located in the music room inside the stage right tunnel, directed the principal characters. All departments worked independently for three days.

Rehearsal for *Peter Pan,* 1992.

During this time the technical crew engaged in a variety of activities. Stage managers attended some of the rehearsals, lighting assistants plotted light cues, prop men (who had already received the list of props from the set designer) scoured the town searching for items needed for the following week's show, the costume department busily tailored the rented clothing to fit the Starlight characters. The stagehands met and discussed where each scenery wagon needed to go and in what order to move them so as not to create a traffic jam during performance. The paint shop prepared next week's scenery.

Thursday a "put-together" rehearsal took place. Five hours was allotted to go through the entire show. Friday offered a run-through and "clean up" rehearsal. On Saturday morning, the producer saw the whole show for the first time. His comments or additions were noted and incorporated in the late Saturday night (Dracula) rehearsal. Actors took Saturday afternoons off. While they were gone from the theatre, the musicians gathered on the singers' pavilion for a run-through of the music (generally the first time any of them had seen the score). A complete dress rehearsal would take place on Saturday night from midnight to 5 o'clock Sunday morning. At this rehearsal, light intensity and focus was set and sound levels were adjusted for the new performers. Early on Sunday morning, after the cast had been dismissed, the

THE STORY OF STARLIGHT THEATRE

production personnel gathered in the producer's office for final notes and comments.

After the all-night Saturday rehearsal, performers took Sunday morning off, then assembled on Sunday afternoon for an all-music rehearsal with the live orchestra on the singers' pavilion. Mid-day music rehearsals were not conducted on the main stage due to the extreme heat.

For the first twenty-one years of Starlight's existence, actors, singers, dancers and production personnel kept this rigorous schedule in addition to giving a performance every night of the current show! During the 1970s, though, so many touring companies came through Starlight that this sort of seven-day rehearsal schedule was abandoned. The performers in the touring shows already had lines, songs, and dances learned; moreover, costumes, props, and sometimes even sets were already available.

The return of the locally produced musical in 1981 prompted another overhaul of the rehearsal schedule because the number of shows being produced was far less. At least one week fell in between each production, giving the performers sufficient time to rehearse for the next show. Since the late 1980s, the actors, singers, and dancers have been called in a week before the first production is scheduled. They rehearse that week, then perform the first show the following week. The next week, rehearsal begins for the second show, followed by a week's performance. The west pavilion is still the one used for the singers; dancers use the east pavilion. Performers seldom utilize the main stage for rehearsal unless a large ensemble needs the great space or unless certain sets are incorporated within the routine. The actors work an eight-hour day during rehearsal week. The dress and technical rehearsal takes place on Sunday night from seven until nearly midnight.

The level of expertise of the people behind the scenes accounts for Starlight's professional appearing productions. The directors, actors, singers, and dancers are highly trained. The technical staff is incredibly adept at putting together top quality products under considerable pressure. During the 1950s and 1960s, the continuity of the production staff aided greatly in the ease with which things were planned and executed. (See the Production and Technical Staff listing on page 123). In addition, an enormous amount of pre-planning goes into the upcoming season during the off months.

Starlight Theatre is indeed unique. The overall design, the enormous size, the backstage area, the way in which scenery is constructed and mounted for productions, and the audience area are like no other theatre in this country. The rehearsal schedule followed by those performers and technicians during the first twenty-one years was a grueling one. Starlight established its reputation as one of the best outdoor theatres in the country.

Yet its greatness is not due to the bricks and mortar, the design of the scene wagons or the framework of the canvas flats, the giant-size fan shape of the patrons' seating area, nor to the intense rehearsal schedule. Starlight's prestige is truly due to the sweat and brilliance of the craftsmen, performers, musicians, directors, and producers who devoted their lives to its success. It was so in the beginning.

The Theatre Managers

By mid-twentieth century the Starlight Theatre physical facility was finally taking shape under the capable hands of Kansas City workmen. Sufficient funds, nearly a quarter of a century in accumulating, had become available due to the efforts of many citizens who made the public aware of the need and benefit of a large outdoor theatre. The Starlight Association, a group to guide the theatre policies, was being put into place. What this theatre needed was a producing director, one who knew show business, understood the workings of New York and Hollywood, grasped the complexities of casting, recognized and fostered young actors, actresses, and stage craftsmen, had a vision of what Starlight Theatre was to become, and possessed the power of personality to demand that vision be honored. The search committee went to the New York business quarters of Richard Berger with questions. They left his office with a producing director who stayed at Starlight for twenty-one years and who, more than any other single personality, set the stage and charted the course of professional outdoor theatre in Kansas City.

RICHARD BERGER
(1951–71)

Dick Berger is a man as all men should hope to be—self-educated. Dick was the best educated man I have ever known. He knew how to live and the value of learning from life's experiences. If I were to write his epitaph, it would be the saying which Dick frequently quoted to me, "Once you know—you know forever."

Joseph Bird Hall, longtime friend of Richard Berger, and grandson of one of the founders of the Emery, Bird, Thayer department store in Kansas City.

Left: **A scene** from *Man of La Mancha*, 1974.

DAMN YANKEES • FANNY • HAPPY HUNTING • ROSALINDA • TOM SAWYER •THE MOST HAPPY FELLA • THE BELLS ARE RINGING • LI'L ABNER • WEST SIDE STORY • MEET ME IN ST. LOUIS • DESTRY RIDES AGAIN • RED HEAD • CINDERELLA • CALAMITY JANE • TAKE ME ALONG • FLOWER DRUM SONG • THE MUSIC MAN • AROUND THE WORLD IN EIGHTY DAYS • FIORELLO • BYE BYE BIRDIE • WILDCAT • CARNIVAL • THE UNSINKABLE MOLLY BROWN • MY FAIR LADY • MILK AND HONEY • TOVARICH • MR. PRESIDENT • LITTLE ME •

Richard Berger.

The power and the force behind Starlight Theatre was Dick Berger.
Jerry Funk, former stage manager at Starlight Theatre, and owner of Backstage Workshop in Kansas City, Missouri.

Dick Berger was a magnificent rogue. You'd love him in spite of himself.
Aldon Ferrara, son of and former assistant to the second general manager at Starlight Theatre.

"'Genius' was the word they used in the newspaper review," chuckled Richard Berger in the fall of 1989 when he was interviewed in his Los Angeles apartment. In 1937 he had assembled the cast of performers for the annual Jubilesta fall festival held in Kansas City's Municipal Auditorium. The news article's mention of "genius" in reference to Berger's abilities had sent the Starlight search committee off to New York to track him down. Berger had introduced them to three or four other directors as possible Starlight candidates. The committee, however, was interested in him.

Bill Symon was a part of that committee, and, from the beginning, Starlight was blessed with the talents of those two men. Both powerful, both forces to be reckoned with, both generally stayed out of each other's way. Berger, from the very inception of his contract, was the absolute dictator of the theatre's artistic side. Symon became the unquestioned money man, dutifully guarding the finances, promoting the Starlight image throughout the community, and at times running interference to keep certain persons out of Berger's realm. The theatre has not had that same sort of management team since Bill Symon's death in 1966.

Berger's theatrical experience went back to 1927 when he quit Central High School to become the ticket boy in the Forty-sixth Street Theatre in New York. Oddly enough, tennis opened the door to some important lifelong connections. During those early decades of the twentieth century, a fellow was considered "sissy" if caught on the streets of New York with a tennis racket in his hand. So Berger, an avid tennis player, would hide his racket inside his shirt while going to and from the courts. He didn't have to hide his racket, though, at the theatre. In fact, it was as the fourth man in a doubles tennis match that he met Oscar Hammerstein II. The two men crossed paths many times throughout their careers.

It was also at the Forty-sixth Street Theatre that Berger was befriended by Lawrence Schwab of the Schwab and Mandel producing firm. When that firm dissolved, Schwab accepted a job as production director for the St. Louis Municipal Opera. He took Berger with him as his assistant when the man originally selected refused to fly to the new job. Two years later, when Schwab retired, Berger filled the position.

At the Muny, Berger learned a philosophy of theatre that he brought with him to Starlight: large public theatres were places for family entertainment. Racy nightclub

acts and risqué plays thus had no room in the Starlight bookings. In 1970, Berger remarked that he doubted Starlight would ever produce such shows as *Hair* or *Oh! Calcutta!* or *Futz*. The theatre had a reputation for family entertainment and Berger thought that's what the patrons wanted. He intended to keep it that way.

Richard Berger and Jeanne Bal in *Peter Pan,* 1956.

The Theatre Managers

25

Dorothy Coulter, the most frequently seen leading lady on the Starlight stage.

It was, and remains today, very expensive to mount shows in New York. Oftentimes producers and writers will choose to open a show in another town to try out the new material, work out problems, make additions, or, in some cases, scuttle the whole production. At the Muny, Berger exercised the same single-minded determination to mold his theatre for which he was later known at Starlight. For example, during the pre-New York run of a new production of *Gentlemen Unafraid* (written by Oscar Hammerstein, Otto Harbach, and Jerome Kern), Max Gordon, who was to be the director of the Broadway version, wanted Buddy Ebsen to play the role of Bud Hutchins. Berger, however, had just seen a promising young talent whom he preferred for his production. He told Max that selecting a Broadway cast was Max's prerogative, but for St. Louis, Berger wanted this young fellow Red Skelton. Skelton got the job.

Berger's association with the St. Louis theatre lasted eight years. Then he was off to Hollywood, where Louis Mayer was looking for young non-draftable directors. Mayer sent a limousine to pick him up and deliver him to the studio, where he signed a one-year contract. Berger later moved to RKO, where he made several motion pictures, including *Rachel and the Stranger* and *Roughshod*. Berger returned to New York to produce the Perry Como show for the fledgling television industry. He also secured the job of director at NBC by a show of wily ingenuity. Berger told the sponsors that, as producer, he had decided to hire himself as the show's director. When they objected, he showed them the clause in the contract stating that as producer he could select his own director; he chose himself.

Berger was a successful television director, but the hectic pace and potential ulcers made him reconsider his choice of professions. When the Starlight offer came to him, he and his wife Sherry decided that a slower tempo might be desirable. Sherry, a former Ziegfeld girl, was to remain his lifelong partner until her death in July 1975. According to Phil de Rosier, Sherry "was a gorgeous, warm, loving human being" who supported Berger's decision to move with their young son to this town called Kansas City and begin another career as an outdoor theatre producer with an unknown and untried group.

Berger accepted the Starlight position on these terms: first, it would be a twelve-month position, four of which he would spend in Kansas City, eight of which he could spend in New York, at his Florida home, or wherever he chose. Second, he would maintain a full-time office in New York with a full-time secretary. The contract was the first signed by the Starlight Theatre Association. For the opening production, Berger chose *The Desert Song* by Sigmund Romberg and the composer himself was on hand to conduct the overture.

In those early years, the season consisted of ten shows that included a mixture of operettas, light opera, and new musical comedies recently written for the Broadway stage. *The Chocolate Soldier* and *Naughty Marietta* from the 1951 season remain in the top two dozen musicals of Starlight's history (see the Starlight Awards on page

The Story of Starlight Theatre

107). *Babes in Toyland*, also presented that same year, was the first of a series of children's shows that featured young Kansas Citians.

Berger frequently brought New York talent to Kansas City audiences, sometimes casting the same performer who had played the role on Broadway. Berger also chose local talent when quality was apparent. The most frequently seen leading actress on the Starlight stage throughout its history was Dorothy Coulter. Lilian Armijo, a member of the singing ensemble, holds the record for the most performances for supporting roles by an actress. Both of these women were and remain today residents of Kansas City.

Berger produced the first opera, *Carmen*, in 1954, the first variety show, "Liberace," in 1957, and a world premier of *Tom Sawyer* in 1958. The 1960 season brought the first touring book musical show to Starlight audiences, *West Side Story*. Michael Bennett, who later created *A Chorus Line*, was the dance captain of that show.

The opening musical for the 1956 season (*Peter Pan*, starring Jeanne Bal) demanded more technical preparation than a show usually requires. Assembling the machinery necessary to take Peter and his friends airborne consumed many hours. The original machinery used in London's 1904 production was developed by George Kirby. Joseph Kirby inherited the family secret, and when the new musical version arrived on Broadway in 1954, a young Englishman named Peter Foy supervised the apparatus for the Kirby family. Foy came to Starlight for the same purpose. Berger wanted to be certain that the "darn thing would fly," so he insisted on being the first one to try out the new cables. Satisfied that all was well, he and Jeanne Bal got an aerial tour of the Starlight backstage facilities.

A performance in the 1958 season offered the unusual idea of building a stage out over the orchestra pit to bring a performer closer to the audience. The performer was Jerry Lewis, who, after the Monday night opening, had decided that he couldn't get much audience rapport because he was too far away from the people. He took his idea of building a new stage to Berger, and the two of them in turn went to Symon who proceeded to tell Mr. Lewis that the cost of such an addition stretched beyond Starlight's allowed budget. Lewis had the stage built and paid for it out of his own pocket.

The first world premiere presented at Starlight was *Tom Sawyer* in July 1958. Berger had gotten the idea for making a musical in December of 1957 when he and his wife were in Florida. She was preparing for a music program and was listening to records of the music produced for the 1956 U.S. Steel Hour's *Tom Sawyer*. Upon hearing the delightful melodies, Berger recognized the makings of a musical play. He contacted Edward Reveaux, stage director at Starlight in 1951 and 1952, who was a former professor of play production at Yale University's Baker Workshop. They in turn contacted Peter Gurney, a student at the Yale School of Drama, and the three of them wrote and rewrote a script that retained the flavor and humor of the original novel. The score had been written by Frank Luther, a native of Lakin, Kansas, with over six hundred tunes to his

PHOTO COURTESY OF STARLIGHT THEATRE

Lilian Armijo, the most frequently seen supporting actress on the Starlight stage.

Right: **Bobby Rydell** in *Tom Sawyer,* 1964.

Below: **Phil de Rosier** and friends in front of the Twain museum in Hannibal, Missouri.

credit. Luther had composed the original music for very few instruments, so Roland Fiore, the musical director at Starlight for eighteen years, had to re-orchestrate the entire score to fit his thirty-five piece orchestra. In May of that year, Berger and Phil de Rosier traveled to Hannibal, Missouri to inspect Tom's real cave and to get a feel for the genuine flavor of the community. The show was quite successful and returned to Starlight the next year in 1959, then in 1964, and again in 1970.

Around the World in Eighty Days in 1962 became the most technically difficult show thus far produced. Among other things, the technical staff had to find a live Indian elephant capable of doing specific stage business and an ostrich willing to pull a cart. The carpentry crew, headed by Ancel Lacy, was challenged to build a railroad car that would hold a score of passengers and be sturdy enough for a band of "Indians" to run across the top of it. Lacy's crew also had to construct a steamship that could be completely dismantled each night. The script called for everything, from the masts to the figurehead and the cabin to the paddle wheel, to be thrown into the ship's boiler to provide fuel. Now, add to all those problems the challenge of assembling a giant crane to hoist the balloon up over the audience area, and the

THE STORY OF STARLIGHT THEATRE

many sighs of relief heard for a week following the opening performance can be appreciated!

By 1962 the number of shows was cut down to eight each season, with three shows having a two-week run, one at the start of the season, one in the middle, one at the end. The need to alleviate the constant stress of mounting weekly shows accounted for the rescheduling. A two-week "breather" was healthy medicine for an exhausted crew and staff.

During those early years, Starlight had tremendous community support, very much perceived as "the place to be." The local newspaper gave considerable space to the young theatre, and the local critic, Landon Laird, rallied to the cause of Starlight more than once. As reported by Berger thirty-eight years later, "You can only aspire to a certain level of perfection in one week. A hard-lined critic could have killed Starlight in two weeks—well, a year anyway."

The early 1950s saw a shortage of performers, especially male performers, due to the Korean War. Many of the first seasons' principals doubled in another show as principal characters. Later in the fifties, Berger developed a "star system." He would sometimes hire a well-known singer who had never played a lead in a book show and give him or her the chance to perform on the Starlight stage, such as Vic Damone in *The Great Waltz* (1959), Johnny Desmond in *Say, Darling* (1959), Carol Burnett in *Calamity Jane* (1961), John Davidson in *Camelot* (1965), John Gary in *She Loves Me*, (1965), and Marilyn Maye in *Hello, Dolly!* in (1970). He also gave Dom de Luise his first break on an outdoor theatre stage. Berger had seen him perform in a little theatre at New York's McAlpin Hotel and decided that he was the one to play the lead comic Mr. Fix role in Starlight's 1962 production of *Around the World in Eighty Days.*

Berger would also hire entertainers to interpolate and sometimes interrupt the dramatic action with their special acts. In the 1955 presentation of *Cole Porter Festival*, the show-stopping act of the festival was Hal LeRoy's dance to "Tea for Two." According to Landon Laird, the audience loved it. The trouble was that Cole Porter didn't write "Tea For Two." Vincent Youmans did.

Berger also had a knack for adding the unusual to enhance the pizzazz of his shows. Former President Harry Truman, who resided in Independence, Missouri, occasionally came to the theatre as an audience member. In the summer of 1964, however, he came as a performer. Berger had asked Mr. Truman to make

The Theatre Managers

Above: **Ed Reveaux**, stage director at Starlight in 1952 and 1953.
Below: **Starlight carpenters** Woody Brumett and John Hogan constructing the steamship for *Around the World in Eighty Days.*

PHOTO COURTESY OF STARLIGHT THEATRE

Marilyn Maye, *Hello, Dolly!* 1970.

a guest appearance on the first night of *Mr. President* and play himself in the role of the president. Mr. Truman agreed to make his theatrical debut, but, as fate would have it, an attack of appendicitis forced him into an ambulance during the intermission.

The list of name stars who graced the stage of Starlight during those years is a long one (see the Show Chronology on p.109). Sterling Holloway, Hal LeRoy, Gisele MacKenzie, Dorothy Coulter, Jeanette MacDonald, Howard Keel, Julie Wilson, Gale Gordon, Tony Bennett, Bill Hayes, Victoria Sherry, Shirley Jones, Pat Suzuki, Frankie Laine, Anna Maria Alberghetti, Gogi Grant, Vic Damone, Gordon and Sheila MacRae, Forrest Tucker, Chita Rivera, Gregory Hines, Brenda Lee, Carol Burnett, Dan Dailey, Martha Raye, Al Hirt, Don Ameche, Jack Jones, Cyd Charisse, Arthur Godfrey, Cab Calloway, Donald O'Connor, Ginger Rogers, and Ethel Merman—these names represent just a partial list of the performers who entertained Kansas City audiences during the years 1951-1971.

Berger had a very hard-line philosophy when it came to his theatre. Berger's stage manager, Jerry Funk, cites an example:

> *Berger was sometimes obsessed with the need to be on top of everything—to be perceived as totally in control and in command of all aspects of the productions. Berger, as well as the designer, director, and choreographer, did not attend all performances nor was it necessary for them to be at the theatre every night. One evening a member of the Board of Directors happened to be backstage and overheard the fact that one of the principal cast members had not appeared by the half-hour call and the understudy was being prepared to go on in his place. The episode turned out to be uneventful as the missing actor showed up just before curtain time, much to the relief of a very anxious understudy. However, the board member left the theatre and went to a restaurant where he accidentally ran into Berger and told him about the backstage problem. Berger was furious that the board member could know something that he didn't. He dashed off to the theatre, arriving there at intermission. He quickly tracked me down and instructed me: In the future, if someone backstage gets stabbed, the first thing you will do is call me.* <u>Then</u> *you can pull out the knife.*

Another example of Berger's theatre philosophy emerged in 1970 as he was describing the ill fates and ill winds that could ruin a performance. When speaking of the band Paul Revere and the Raiders, the first rock group to appear at Starlight, Berger said, "These rock 'n' roll groups have all this fancy electrical equipment. One

THE STORY OF STARLIGHT THEATRE

drop of rain on it and zap—they're all dead, electrocuted. Then where's my show? Oh please don't let it rain."

Despite all the laughs, despite all the glamour and glitz, despite all the stars and bright lights, theatre is, when it is all said and done, a business; and business-wise, in the latter part of the 1960s, Starlight was losing money. In 1970 a plea went out to the community for underwriting money critical for the salvation of the theatre. *The Kansas City Times* proclaimed that "the theatre has been a vital force in the life of this area for 19 years and has entertained millions of adults and children during its lifetime. To permit it to fall by the wayside is unthinkable." The summer of 1969 had been a wet one. Six performances were canceled and patrons had stayed away many more nights due to the threat of rain. The theatre faced a $150,000 shortfall. The first pledges solicited by Symon's group at the theatre's opening had been called in by 1957. Funds derived from a second campaign mounted the next year had been spent by 1969.

The cost of name performers also began skyrocketing. With the rise in television's popularity, performers could do a guest spot or a role in an hour-long play, a matter of one or two days' work, and earn as much money as they might make in the summer theatre for a week of rehearsals and seven performances.

Former President and Mrs. Truman with Hildegarde, *Can Can*, 1957.

PHOTO COURTESY OF STARLIGHT THEATRE

Further, audience tastes were changing and the number of patrons attending Starlight started dropping. The year 1952 had an attendance figure of 360,511, falling to 359,398 the next season. (The local newspaper reported figures considerably higher—440,000 in 1952; 462,000 in 1953.) The attendance figures according to the Starlight Theatre Association report for the years 1965 and 1966 were 249,362 and 284,689, respectively. Also during the early 1950s, the average cost of mounting a show per week was approximately $55,000. In 1971 the average cost per week for eleven weeks was $100,581.23, an increase of close to 83%. As

The Theatre Managers

Starlight came to rely more and more on the touring prepackaged shows. Amidst rising budgets and shrinking revenues, a resident producing director was viewed as an unnecessary luxury. After the 1971 summer season, the Starlight Theatre Board and its president asked Berger to retire. At the time he was sixty-six years old, had a home in the Florida Keys, enjoyed good health, and decided to leave show business behind him.

In 1989, Berger, an eighty-five-year-old theatre veteran, reminisced about his years. He was asked if having it to do all over, would he still have come to Starlight. His answer was AB-SO-LUTE-LY! He adamantly admitted that the Starlight years were some of the best of his life.

Berger continued his upbeat perspective on life well into his eighth decade. At the age of eighty-six, he entered into his second marriage. This time he chose a Los Angeles woman, Natalie Wurderman.

During his early years in St. Louis, Berger had the unfortunate experience of being replaced by someone else on short notice. Realizing then that show business was an idiotic industry, he decided to go out and have a silver bullet made with his initials on it. He vowed that if his experiences in the business ever got too crazy, he might force himself to make use of it. Sitting on the sofa in his California apartment, Berger fingered the silver bullet lovingly and with a smile proclaimed, "Well, I've never had to use it." Lucky for him—lucky for thousands of Kansas Citians who enjoyed some great musical theatre in the 1950s, 1960s and early 1970s.

WILLIAM SYMON
(1951-66)

On the flip side of the managerial coin during the first years of Starlight's existence stood the powerful figure of William Symon. He was a rare man whose prodigious amounts of work went unnoticed at the time but resulted in outstanding achievements. Symon preferred to work behind the scenes rather than in the limelight. He was shrewd, energetic, aggressive, and likable, never allowing his enthusiasm to get out of bounds and lead him into impractical projects. He endured as the perfect foil to a man like Dick Berger.

When Bill Symon came to the post of business director at Starlight, he arrived with a long list of civic accomplishments, including terms as the executive manager of the Kansas City, Missouri Chamber of Commerce, the Citizens' Regional Planning Council, and the Kansas City Art Institute. Aside from his official positions, he had been responsible for obtaining and assisting in the handling of the 1921 National American Legion Convention and the 1928 Republican National Convention; financing the original NCAA Basketball Tournament; and, managing the city bond campaign of 1947 that provided funds for

William Symon.

the beginning of Starlight. He had served, too, as the unpaid manager of the Kansas City Philharmonic Orchestra for eight years.

In 1951 Richard Fowler wrote a book entitled *Leaders in Our Town*. In it he stated that

> *for about 30 years Scottish-born Bill Symon has been the professional organizer of civic Kansas City. His story in detail would tell a large part of the story of big Kansas City projects since the year 1920. Yet few persons beyond the leaders of each enterprise have understood what Bill Symon did to make them succeed. There has been no secret about his Kansas City work, but usually it is backstage. In Kansas City history he is the man who rounds up the leaders and speech makers and builds the organizations. Given the Symon touch big undertakings succeed with amazing regularity.*

TICKET COURTESY OF BARBARA THORNE

Symon and the publicity office he oversaw took responsibility for a wide variety of activities designed to get the Kansas City community involved in the theatre. In 1956 visitors toured the backstage area and watched a rehearsal of *Peter Pan*. They were the first such guests ever to witness a Starlight rehearsal. Symon occasionally conducted tours himself for visiting dignitaries. Organizers formed a women's group in 1956 to acquaint the members with the workings of the theatre. Mrs. Martha Franklin was named to head this new group. A high school advisory board also founded that year exposed students to theatre operations in the hope that they would interest other students in Kansas City's multimillion dollar project.

Mrs. Ginger Hydeman founded the Women's Committee in 1958. This group has assisted the theatre greatly throughout the years, hosting an annual cast party, conducting an open house each spring at the theatre, providing guided tours, and promoting the sale of season tickets.

News story from *The Kansas City Star,* December 2, 1951.

Jim McQueeny, Symon's head of publicity, became a highly visible agent who helped keep the Starlight image in front of the public. His background and flair had evolved in writing and public relations positions, including the Chicago World's Fair. McQueeny

The Theatre Managers

Leaders In Our Town

For Thirty Years Large Civic Promotions of Kansas City Have Been Guided by William M. Symon's Professional Hand, With Resulting Success for the Convention Bureau, the Philharmonic Orchestra, the City Bond Campaign, the Kansas City Art Institute and the Starlight Theater.

studied and collected thirty notebooks of directives from Barnum and Bailey on "How to Get Kids to Come to the Circus." His ground rules derived from these eminent showmen proved an excellent training course for a public relations man.

McQueeny promoted Starlight by writing articles about the theatre's early history and stories about the visiting stars. He would pick up the celebrities from the airport, talk with them, and soon have an article available to the press. He would take them around town to visit "the man on the street" in restaurants, at club meetings, in hospitals, and at several department stores. These personal touches were very important to Kansas Citians who, in an age before mass television, had limited access to star performers. McQueeny continuously enhanced the aura of Starlight as *the* place to go.

Symon had numerous city connections as well as many on the state level. Berger may have known New York, but Symon knew Kansas City. If a problem arose, he knew where to call for answers. He solved not only financial dilemmas but, at times, theatrical ones too. When Phil de Rosier expressed concerns in 1962 about rigging the huge crane for the balloon and basket in *Around the World in Eighty Days,* Symon was on the phone immediately and, according to de Rosier, "in a matter of three minutes had contacted the right people in Cleveland, Ohio, who later came to Starlight and assembled the crane. He knew everybody— that's just the way it was."

William Symon and Richard Berger in front of the temporary stage for *The Jerry Lewis Show,* 1958.

Symon respected Dick Berger but did not hold him in awe; thus the two of them represented a strong team. Symon had managed the first Kansas City Jubilesta, the festival that prompted the "genius" review calling attention to Berger's abilities. One can only assume that Symon knew Berger, approved of his work, and actively promoted his hiring as producing director. In a 1966 article entitled "Bill Symon's Civic Success," *The Kansas City Times* summarized his pivotal position: "An inevitable part of any theatrical enterprise is some friction between business-office budget realities and the soaring imaginations of talented, creative artists. He walked that tightrope ably, sometimes shouting, sometimes soothing, until agreements were reached that profitably solved the classic show business dilemma: 'It's art, but will it sell?'"

Symon had been born in Dunfermline, Scotland, also the birthplace of Andrew Carnegie. When the steel magnate paid a visit to his hometown one year, he noticed the drawings of Symon's father and told him "If you want to come to America when you are a man, I will have a job waiting for you." Symon's father remembered these words and brought his family across the Atlantic when young Bill was two years old. Employment in the steel mills ended with a strike barely two months after his being hired, so Symon's father took a job with the railroad and settled the family in Brookfield, Missouri. Later the family moved to the larger town of St. Joseph.

There, in his high school years, Symon exhibited the wise but thrifty side of his personality. Active in a variety of sports programs, he also had his eye on the tenor part for the senior class play, perhaps because Dorothy Nash, a pretty classmate, was playing the female lead part. However, another male student wanted the tenor part badly enough to pay five dollars. Bill pocketed the money and stepped aside. Later, however, he married the attractive Dorothy and was five dollars richer in the bargain!

Symon attended the University of Missouri, where he very nearly flunked the public speaking course. The man who addressed hundreds of civic groups throughout his professional career simply couldn't get too interested in trying to arouse a classroom of fellow students. Symon left the university to serve in World War I. After the war, he came to Kansas City and worked as a newspaperman for *The Kansas City Times*. Two years later he joined the staff of the Chamber of Commerce and began a life's work of community contributions.

Bill Symon conducting a backstage tour.

After a long and successful marriage that produced one son, Symon's wife Dorothy died. He remarried, this time to a Kansas City woman, Margaret Lish, who outlived him by twenty-three years.

When Symon died in January 1966, Landon Laird's "About Town" column in *The Kansas City Times* included the same sentiment expressed by Mr. Fowler fifteen years earlier—whenever proposals arose, "Symon went forward with detailed recommendations, projected budgets, organizational charts, and other devices he utilized in pinning civic dreams to paper."

The efforts of John Moore and the Centennial Committee coupled with the strengths of Symon's extensive background in community affairs provided a solid base of support for a young, struggling theatre. The success of Starlight Theatre in no small way stemmed directly from Bill Symon's efforts, a fact that, characteristically, he probably would not have admitted publicly.

ANTHONY FERRARA
(1972–80)

When William Symon passed away in January of 1966, he left Starlight's financial affairs in the hands of Tony Ferrara. Ferrara had been a part of Starlight's history since the opening season; his was the second contract signed by the Starlight Association in 1951. He came to the theatre first as an assistant lighting coordinator and later as stage manager before transferring into the business department.

Ferrara was a person trained in the fine arts, and music was a tradition in his family.

PHOTO COURTESY OF ALDON FERRARA

Anthony Ferrara.

His Sicilian grandfather was a tenor who toured with Shubert and with the circus, his grandmother played musical instruments as well as sang, and his own father, Dominique Ferrara, toured the United States as a singer for sixteen years before settling in Jackson County. He was known as "The Kansas City Caruso."

When Tony Ferrara was five years old, he began violin lessons on a half-size violin. He also became a boy soprano. He first performed professionally at age eight, collecting $40 for singing two consecutive nights at Fairyland Park. His high school years were taken up with the love and study of music. His parents owned a restaurant/nightclub on Highway 40, and he and his close friend Arthur Adelman would go out to the club often. Young Ferrara and his father would sing to the customers, fortunate enough on those evenings to enjoy excellent music along with delicious food. Even just driving around town he would sing the famous arias from operas he loved so dearly and would ask his friend Arthur to comment on his progress. Eventually enrolling to study voice at the Conservatory of Music, there his lusty and powerful voice began to develop.

Ferrara traveled to New York for further study. He had auditioned for the Metropolitan Opera and hoped an operatic career was in store for him when the fateful events of December 7, 1941, changed his life's plans. Within two months this budding performer was on a transport ship in the Pacific. He ended up in Australia, entertaining the soldiers and making broadcasts to U.S. troops in the Pacific. Here in the subcontinent he met his wife, Juanita Margaret Bell (Nita), who was working with the Australian Broadcasting Commission. She shared his love for music as well as his devotion to a family. Together they reared four children, all of whom have chosen the theatre business as their life's work.

After the war, Ferrara returned to New York to try to resurrect a singing career. The five-year interruption of voice training brought about by the war, however, did not work to his advantage. Most performing jobs were taken by singers and musicians who had continued working during the war. As supporting a family on the small funds he could have received from performing was simply not possible, he decided to find another type of job in the theatre world. Ferrara loved the world of performers, yet he somehow felt that he had been "cursed with a beautiful voice." According to his friend Arthur Adelman, if Ferrara hadn't had such a beautiful voice, he might have been more content with his lot; but, because of that unfulfilled talent, he felt he had missed the top rung of the opera world where he sensed his destiny to have been.

Ferrara's first Starlight summers were spent on the light bridge giving lighting cues. In 1954 he rose to the assistant stage manager position and rode the curtain every night of performance. When Ferrara entered the business office, he not only worked within the confines of that space but he also conducted annual tours of Starlight's backstage as part of a seminar for local high school students. He often traveled

THE STORY OF STARLIGHT THEATRE

around the Kansas City area speaking to civic groups about Starlight's successes and its upcoming season.

When Ferrara assumed the command position at Starlight, he was acutely aware that artistic tastes had to be paid for in hard cash. Ferrara once remarked to a newspaper reporter that "many theatres around the country have been closed by following the premise that the artistic aspect of a production is all that needs to be considered. A prime consideration must be money to pay the bills." For the first years of the theatre's existence, the eternal battle of art versus finances was waged by two men, each guarding his bailiwick and each kept in check by the other. When Berger left the theatre, the positions of producer and business manager were combined; thus, for Ferrara, there was no counterpart to help with the immense job of scheduling shows, overseeing the productions, promoting the Starlight image, soothing the often demanding temperaments of visiting stars, guarding the finances, and most importantly, helping to facilitate decisions with the Starlight Board. The management team that had molded Starlight and made it so successful in its first years was replaced by a solo performer who was expected to walk the tightrope of both jobs equally well.

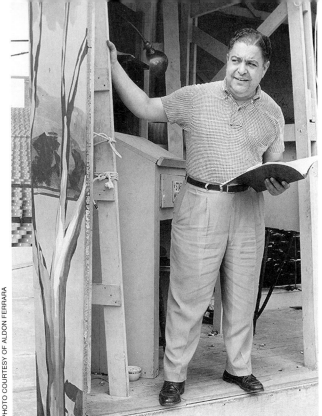

Above: **Tony Ferrara** riding the curtain as stage manager.

Left: **Tony Ferrara** conducting a backstage tour, 1960.

Above: **Carol Channing**, *Hello, Dolly!*, 1977.

Below: **Jim Nabors**, star of the second most popular variety show in Starlight's history.

Shortly after Ferrara became the general manager, he brought his son Aldon to the theatre as his assistant. The younger man had been working near Canton, Ohio, at the Canal Fulton Theatre, a dinner theatre attached to a restaurant. He began in his father's employment as operations manager; there was no assistant general manager position at the time. Aldon's brother Mark was hired to work in Starlight's public relations department several years later.

The three Ferraras would ride to work together each day, laughing, haggling, or hotly conversing about some theatre issue. At quitting time, father and sons would return to the car and sometimes resume the same conversation they had left unfinished that morning. One evening Tony was especially tired, and when the words started to flow about some minor point left unsaid from the A.M. discussion, he despaired, "Is there no peace?" Occasionally, to really cause a steamy debate, Mark Ferrara would impishly suggest that Starlight produce *The Pajama Game*, a musical he knew both his brother and father despised and thought too dated. Good-humored repartee would result, each man knowing that the other two just wanted a lively exchange to cap off the day.

All three Ferraras loved the theatre business—especially the Starlight Theatre business. They shared a common experience and kept their own counsel. According to Mark Ferrara, the two sons whose acquaintance with Starlight had begun years earlier when they were employed as wash boys and envelope stuffers felt "very fortunate to have been around early in Starlight's beginnings and to have worked with professionals like Dick Berger, Roland Fiore, and director Bert Yarborough, all of whom had experience which took them back to the origins of musical theatre in America."

The Ferrara years were times of transition for the theatre. The final season under Berger had been artistically sound but financially disastrous. In the years that followed, Ferrara and the Starlight Board decided to offer seasons of variety shows only. Gone were the lavish sets and beautiful melodies of the earlier operettas, the popular musical comedies, the choruses of young and talented Kansas City hopefuls, and the rich lyrical sounds of the Starlight orchestra.

The theatre needed revenue. Simply stated, the operation made money with the variety shows and lost money with the book musicals. From the mid-1960s to the mid-1970s, the average book musical lost $5,740 a week, while twenty-nine weeks of star variety shows recorded an average profit of $7,750 a week. Throughout the 1970s, when the theatre acquired money from its variety show format, the return of the book musical sapped that extra cash flow from the coffers.

In 1975, attendance figures were cited as an indication that Starlight was in trouble. The 1975 season's total was 233,715, down more than 15,000 from 1965. The lower attendance figure apparently resulted from differences of artistic taste. John

Haskins, writing for *The Kansas City Star*, reported in September 1975 that "it is a perennial consideration in theatrical ventures, of course, where it is accepted as immutable law that costs always rise while ticket prices remain stable. Counterbalancing this attitude is the belief of experienced theatrical folk that the money is the easiest part of it, while the hard part is bringing off the finished product artistically. People will pay for good things, and they stay away in droves from things that do not measure up to expectations."

Above: **Mitzi Gaynor** entertaining at Starlight, 1973.
Below: **Yul Brynner**, *The King and I*, 1976.

The people of Kansas City missed the book musicals whether the shows lost money or not. For twenty-one years audiences had expected to see those kinds of shows at Starlight, and when they were no longer being offered, there was grumbling. "Why should we go to Starlight and pay money to see a show that many times isn't as good as something that can be found easily on television?" asked a reader in *The Kansas City Times* column "Speaking the Public Mind." In an article titled "Starlight Needs Some Change," the newspaper offered some blunt advice: "this fine Kansas City civic enterprise needs to learn from its continuing experience every year, and another disappointing season with virtually all TV star package shows suggests some revision to bring fresh appeal."

What many community people did not understand was that the decision to abandon the book musicals reflected financial judgment, not an assessment of artistic merit. It was one of the hardest decisions Tony Ferrara ever had to make. According to his son Aldon, Tony was tortured for days before making the announcement because he knew it was a changing era and that he would be criticized for his choice. Thoroughly conscious of the artistic deficiencies of TV-type package shows, though, he tried to rectify the situation.

A year preceding Starlight's silver anniversary in 1975 the book musical made a reappearance on the Swope Park stage. *Man of La Mancha* was followed the next year by *Carousel* and *The Wizard of Oz* with Margaret Hamilton reprising her movie role of the Wicked Witch. The 1976 season included eight musicals. Jan Peerce starred in *Fiddler on the Roof*, Angela Lansbury was featured in *Mame* (she also returned two years later to play Mama Rose in *Gypsy*), and Yul Brynner entertained Starlight patrons with his performance of a strong and willful Siamese king in *The King and I*. The following year Carol Channing charmed Kansas City audiences

with her rendition of *Hello, Dolly!* and *The Sound of Music* starring Shirley Jones became the second best attended musical in Starlight's history (see Starlight Awards on p.107). However, because Starlight did not produce these shows, the theatre was not in the same position to control the quality of what went on its stage as it had been during the 1950s and 1960s. The same holds true throughout the 1980s and 1990s for those shows that tour through Kansas City but are not produced at the theatre.

During the Ferrara years, Starlight developed new and better ways to make ticket buying easier. A WATTS line was installed at the theatre, 142 outlets sprang up in five states, and 145 companies within the Kansas City area had company agents who actually sold tickets and handled the money.

In 1979 a blue-ribbon committee went searching for a marketing director. Headed by Bob Zimmerman, chairman of the board of the Kansas City Power and Light Company, this group recommended hiring Mark Ferrara, already serving in that capacity unofficially. However, Earnest Dick, the Starlight Theatre Association president, dismissed the recommendation and hired his own research company, the Lawrence Leiter Company, to find the perfect person. Their candidate, Kansas Citian Robert Rohlf, was engaged to fill the position and is now the general manager of Starlight.

Bill Symon once commented that on a board of directors, "everyone has two businesses—his own and show business." The day-to-day conflicts with certain board members proved to be the hardest part of Ferrara's job. Ferrara's old friend, Arthur Adelman, remarked that "when you're dealing with a board of directors who work for a non-profit organization and who make no money for their efforts, everyone thinks they're a genius. The politics were tremendous." Running an outdoor theatre has an entirely different set of problems than managing an indoor one; Starlight's size, the weather, the short season, the mix of shows, and the costs demanded different considerations. Basic philosophical differences also divided the board members.

An example of those differing philosophies occurred with the split decision in mid-season 1980 to lower ticket prices to two-for-one for the last three shows of the season, based on the premise that such a discount would fill empty seats. Assuming that an empty theatre is

Top opposite: **Shirley Jones** starring in *The Sound of Music*, 1977, the second most popular musical in Starlight's history.

Bottom opposite: **Jan Peerce**, *Fiddler on the Roof,* 1976.

Below: **Angela Lansbury** in *Gypsy*, 1978.

PHOTO COURTESY OF STARLIGHT THEATRE

THE STORY OF STARLIGHT THEATRE

like an overstocked rack of clothes, some board members wanted to put the tickets on sale to "get rid of extra inventory." The Ferrara council, however, countered that for an entertainment enterprise like Starlight, a particular show would be seen by those who wanted to see it and the price was of little consequence as long as it was within reach. Anyone disinterested wouldn't pay six cents to go spend an evening in Swope Park. Moreover, what about those season ticket holders who received only a twenty percent discount for buying a season pass? The big two-for-one price break would most certainly insult them. So what if $50,000 was collected from three thousand persons or from six thousand? Starlight had gained nothing. The cost of the show was the same. But the board voted to go ahead with the scheme anyway, and reportedly lost income for the theatre. Trying to gain consensus out of such disharmony required the skills of a political animal. Ferrara wasn't one.

The latter part of the 1970s brought some suggestions to rent the Starlight facility to other performing groups who would be permanent tenants. Ferrara never favored that idea. First, he questioned the wisdom of putting Starlight Theatre in competition with other city performance facilities. Second, if Starlight were going to book rock concerts, why did the theatre need an outside agency to make those arrangements and take a cut of the profits? Also, if Starlight were going to continue with a ten-week season, when would the theatre be available for these touring concerts? The scheduling inevitably would become a nightmare when concerts tried to rearrange their one-or-two-night performance dates when another production was utilizing the stage. Further, interrupting the season sporadically with concerts would break the Starlight tradition of theatrical entertainment every night of the summer.

The mission statement of the theatre reads: "Our mission is to present and/or produce family-oriented quality entertainment at affordable prices." Ferrara always was committed to those concepts. He firmly believed that Starlight should be accessible to the common man, and that the cost of a ticket should not exceed the average person's ability to pay for it.

His overall management style differed markedly from that of Berger's. Whereas Berger had a powerful personality and pushed his ideas to the forefront, Ferrara was much quieter and far less confrontational. Also unlike his predecessor, he had the full responsibility of juggling the finances, coping with the politics of his board as well as overseeing the artistic products presented.

According to figures quoted in the local newspaper, the 1980 season had a dismal attendance figure of 207,000—down 38,000 from 1979 and about 153,000 from five years before. That account disagrees with the Starlight Theatre Association's own figures, though, which indicate that attendance for 1980 had fallen only 2,000 from 1979 and 26,000 from 1975. But when income drops and attendance figures shrink, a change comes about. Somebody is blamed; others see an opportunity. As in the case of Dick Berger before him, Ferrara was asked to leave. He was given twenty-four hours' notice to vacate the theatre to which he had devoted thirty years of his life. He had told his family that among all other considerations, "I want Starlight to be my epitaph." Within six months Tony Ferrara was dead.

ALAN MCCRACKEN
(1981)

The 1981 season brought about a radical change of format for Starlight audiences. The Starlight Association had arranged for the Theatre League and the Kansas City Philharmonic to co-produce the new season, called "Summerfest." The Philharmonic and the Theatre League actually did the producing; the board of directors was to hire the directors, the singers, and dancers, and the actors. The Starlight Theatre's sole role was that of a landlord. This new idea, different from any previous format, was thought to hold limited financial risk.

That season offered four musicals and a series of six three-night concerts featuring guest performers and the Philharmonic orchestra. The Theatre League was responsible for the Broadway musicals while New West and Contemporary Productions, under the supervision of Chris Fritz, oversaw the production of the summer concerts. Alan McCracken, former general manager of Fox Theatre in Atlanta, Georgia, was hired as the new executive manager. His forté, however, was managing historic theatre preservation projects. When McCracken arrived at Starlight, he quickly realized that the complexities of the position exceeded his area of expertise, and he held the job for only one year.

In 1980, 220 members sat on the Starlight Theatre Board. The following year a reorganization pared down the group to only thirty elected officers, with an Executive Committee or Board of Managers to number only seven. Thus the number of decision makers for the theatre fell from nearly ten dozen to under ten. The number of season-ticket holders fell, too. Only thirty-three hundred of 1980's seven thousand renewed their subscriptions.

ROBERT ROHLF
(1982–present)

Another nugget of wisdom often quoted by Bill Symon was "A camel is a horse designed by a committee." Herbert Wilson, a former Starlight Association president, put it another way in an interview with a *Kansas City Times* reporter: "No business can be operated by two or three dozen persons, as we've been operating the Starlight Theatre. That kind of an operation only leads to buck passing when things go wrong. We need a single boss." His remarks, though spoken twenty-four years before Robert Rohlf assumed the position of general manager, remain as true today as the day Wilson spoke them. With Alan McCracken acting as the landlord, plus all the artistic decisions being made either by the Theatre League, by the Board of the Philharmonic, or by New West and Contemporary Productions, and then all of everyone's decisions having to be supervised by the Starlight Association Board of Managers, there were "too many cooks in the kitchen." The whole affair provided a working example of Wilson's statement. A single authority was needed, one who would hire the personnel necessary to produce the shows, plan the seasons, keep the pulse of the business office, and be responsible to Starlight's Board. In 1982 Robert Rohlf was named the general manager.

Robert Rohlf.

Rohlf is a Kansas City business success story. He graduated from Shawnee Mission East High School and Baker University. He had his own auto business for five years and also owned a title insurance company. When the Lawrence Leiter Company conducted the search for a Starlight marketing director in 1980, they made their recommendations known to the Starlight Board, who then offered him the position. Ten years later Rohlf married his administrative assistant at Starlight, Mary Beth Tritt. He has two children by a former marriage.

Rohlf is a businessman in love with Starlight. When he first came to the Swope Park project, he had some misgivings but decided to accept the job anyway. He has never been sorry. He had no inkling in those early years that as the seasons passed he would grow to love the grand theatre as much as his predecessors had.

Why was a businessman appointed to head Starlight? The reasons were expressed most clearly by Bill Culver, the president and CEO of the St. Louis Muny: "The hardest thing for a leader to acquire is financial control and knowledge. A person can acquire theatre know-how from others, but the Chief Executive Officer must know how to handle marketing, money and the board. A good board of directors provides wherewithal to solve problems and helps to fund a project. A good general manager knows how to deal with his board, and knows how to extract their good ideas and utilize them." Rohlf is a person who knows how to market a product, calculate its cost, check the balance sheet, and listen to the people who try to help him. He has taken what was a theatre venture on the brink of financial disaster after the demise of the Kansas City Philharmonic in 1982 and succeeded in making it a glowing and growing

Four Decades of *Show Boat*

The appearance of *Show Boat* in 1927 signaled "the birth of the book musical" as we know it. With its lovely lyrical melodies telling a story of lonely lost romance while daring to breach the racial question in America's history, *Show Boat* served as the reference point for quality and substance for all that came after it. Starlight has presented Jerome Kern and Oscar Hammerstein's musical of life on a Mississippi riverboat six times over the last four decades.

PHOTOS COURTESY OF STARLIGHT THEATRE

Bertha Powell (Queenie) and William C. Smith (who played the role of Joe on Broadway), 1952.

The Dolly Brown Singers, 1957.

1968 production with Arthur Godfrey as Captain Andy.

Robert Horton with Cheryl Clark as Kim, 1963.

44

Shirley Jones (top left) heads the cast of the 1976 production.

Joel Higgins in *Show Boat*, 1992.

Shirley Jones as Magnolia and Ron Husmann as Gaylord Ravenal, 1976.

concern. The 203,728 attendance figure for the four musicals in the 1991 season offers quite a testimonial to Rohlf and his hard-working staff who have fought the uphill financial battle for so long. The struggle hasn't been easy.

Hired in April 1980 to help the dollar-poor theatre, Rohlf's salary for the first three years with Starlight was paid by Hallmark Cards, Inc. When he assumed the duties of general manager, Starlight was in debt—the "six-figure type." The theatre badly needed an influx of cash, or at least a stabilizing lever for cash outlay, if it was going to survive. Rohlf went to each of the fifty-seven creditors and offered them a settlement—25 cents on the dollar. The creditors accepted, and by the end of 1982 Starlight was debt-free.

Being debt-free and having the finances to do the necessary upkeep, though, were two different considerations. In order to raise the money for improvements, several grants were sought. Under a $250,000 challenge grant from the city, Starlight was responsible for repaying $50,000 of the debt. Within the contract was a clause that stated that for every two dollars derived from the private sector, one dollar of the debt would be forgiven up to $200,000. This grant raised $500,000 by the end of 1984.

Another grant, awarded in 1987 by the Parks and Recreation Department, could be summarized simply: "If you help promote the amenities of Swope Park plus form an organization of interested citizens, we'll provide $30,000 a month for four months." With this new source of income, a $2.7 million improvement plan was set in motion. A new stage, updated rehearsal pavilions, and improved backstage food

Above left: **A scene** from *Brigadoon*, 1990.

Below left: **Phyllis Diller** in *The Wizard of Oz*, 1991.

Below right: **Gary Sandy** plays the lead in *The Music Man*, 1992.

Opposite top: **Robert Rohlf**, B. D. Wong, and David Ogden Stiers from *Peter Pan*, 1992.

Opposite bottom: **West Side Story**, 1990.

THE STORY OF STARLIGHT THEATRE

services were planned. The Applause Club, an area adjacent to the east pavil-ion that opens up and provides catering services to small parties and business organizations before a performance, was constructed, as were new walkways, new lighting for the walkways and parking lots, and new public restrooms. All the old wooden seats were replaced.

Since 1983, when Starlight abandoned its caretaker role and assumed the producer's mantle, all production decisions have fallen to the general manag-er. Even though the 1981 season brought a return of the locally produced musical, not every show is produced at Starlight. For example, only two of the four 1991 productions were home grown; touring companies presented the other two. Thus, there is no need for a resident choreographer or a permanent company of singers and dancers. In addition, production personnel are con-tracted for each individual show or, as in the case of the set designer, for each

series of shows in a single season. When concerts play on the Starlight stage, the management acts only as a landlord, not as a producing agent.

Because Rohlf did not grow up immersed in a theatre background, he comes to the job with a fresh eye and an open mind. He never claims expertise in theatre matters. He's honest and straightforward, and allows his crafts-men to exercise their own artistic judgment. He is approachable on a personal and professional level. He can disagree with his directors, yet he can compromise on issues without receiving or giving a bruised ego. His word is final, yet he "knows how to listen. He doesn't make snap decisions," remarked his lighting designer since 1984, Kirk Bookman.

Jack Allison, one of the guest directors at Starlight since 1981, stated, "Bob is more in tune with what his audience wants than any other producer I work with. Unlike most producers who make you think you are working for them, Bob makes you think you're working for the theatre. I feel like I'm performing a public ser-vice instead of doing theatre."

Rohlf does try to reach out to the community and involve them in the glamour of show business. Since 1986, a yearly black-tie gala fund-raiser, held on the Starlight stage, seeks corporate sponsors for each season who will help finance and promote the plays and concerts scheduled. In the late 1980s, another community first for Starlight came in the form of an extra evening's per-formance purchased by US Sprint, filling the entire

Above: **Robert and Mary Beth Rohlf.**

Below: **The Applause Club.**

audience with the company's employees, their families, and friends. Also, in the 1992 season, for the first time in the theatre's history, two locally produced musicals ran for ten days spanning two weekends. These ties to the community bring lifeblood into Starlight and keep the theatre front and center in the public's eye.

In his tenure as general manager, Bob Rohlf has presented not only the traditional musical plays but also the coming of such new fare as *Grease, The Best Little Whorehouse in Texas, Jesus Christ Superstar, Ain't Misbehavin', Annie, Evita, A Chorus Line, Hair, 42nd Street,* and, in 1988, *The Odd Couple*, the first nonmusical play ever presented at Starlight. Since 1982 he has seen the total of season ticket holders increase more than eightfold to an all-time high of 27,000+ for the 1991 season, by the end of which the total attendance figure had also climbed to 11,380,241. The financial turnabout for the theatre has provided one of the most satisfying aspects of his job.

Rohlf began his Starlight career as a person engrossed with steering the ship through troubled financial waters and keeping her afloat. Since he has assumed leadership, Starlight has added millions of dollars of improvements to its facility. On the artistic side, five of the top ten best attended musicals ever presented at Starlight have been on the boards during his tenure (see the Starlight Awards p.107.) Personally he has grown through the years into a true devotee, a man totally committed to the greatness of Starlight and to its future as a showplace and centerpiece for the arts in the Kansas City area. Like his predecessors, he wrestles daily with the question of "Where can Starlight make a difference?" And like the men before him who have held the captain's position, he has charted the dangerous course, agonized over his projections, gripped the wheel during the storms, and come through the tempestuous waters a toughened seaman more in love than ever with the ocean, the boat, and the experience that the journey has afforded.

THE STORY OF STARLIGHT THEATRE

★ INTERMISSION ★

★ When **Dick Berger** was the producing director of Starlight, he was invited by a Dr. Gray of the local Congregational Church to give the homily for a particular Sunday morning. Berger took him up on his offer and went to the service several hours after the closing of rehearsal. His sermon for that day:

> *Some people think that church and theatre don't mix. Church people don't like the strange theatre people and theatre people don't like the stuffy church people. I think we can all get along. Look at it this way. No man beats his dog on Sunday night after Pastor Gray's good sound words from the pulpit. If you came to my theatre on Monday night and saw The Sound of Music, I guarantee you wouldn't go home and beat your dog. Now if we could just find five more shows like The Sound of Music, wouldn't life be great?*

★ In the 1965 touring production of *West Side Story*, **Michael Bennett,** the creator of *A Chorus Line*, was choreographing a dance on stage much to the dislike of **Dick Berger**. They were having an "artistic disagreement." Berger shouted to his stage manager, "Have that kid do it my way or withhold his pay!"

★ During the 1953 run of *Blossom Time*, the backstage personnel saw a few extra sparkling performances when the fireworks they accidentally lit upside down for the finale went flying all over the backstage area. Eleven years later, fireworks presented a similar problem when *Mr. President* was on the boards. **Dick Berger** often quoted the sentiment, "If you start a production big and end it big, what happens in the middle doesn't matter." *Mr. President* had a weak script, so Berger had planned a grand finale with the Boy Scouts marching, the Army Reserve represented, the ensemble dressed in military uniforms, and all flags waving. Fireworks were planned to top off the show. During the late Saturday night "Dracula" rehearsal, the same stagehand (or his cousin) set off the fireworks upside down and sent hundreds of actors scurrying in every which direction. Berger, who witnessed this mess from the audience area, invented a few new words for the English language that evening.

★ In the 1962 production of *Around the World in Eighty Days,* live animals were used for the scenes. At dress rehearsal, an ostrich that was supposed to pull a cart across the stage decided instead it would prefer to chase the director, **Bert Yarborough**, who dashed across the width of the huge stage, jumped off the front of stage right, and proceeded halfway up the audience area before stopping for a breath. Also during

A scene from *The Sound of Music.*

49

The many faces of Joe Macaulay.

rehearsal for the same show, a giant "thud, thud, thud" resounded as the guest elephant walked across the stage. **Dick Berger,** who always had his actors wear rubber on the soles of their shoes to dull the sound of their footsteps, yelled from the audience area, "Put rubber shoes on that — elephant!"

★ In searching for props for *West Side Story,* no one knew that **Al Krikorian,** the property master for Starlight for thirty-one years, had "borrowed" some switchblade knives for the fight scenes from the Kansas City, Missouri, police department. And who knows where he acquired genuine gambling equipment for scenes from *Guys and Dolls?*

★ It was common during Saturday midnight rehearsals for some lighting miscues to occur. By Monday, opening night, the problems usually would be resolved. During the run of 1960's *West Side Story*, though, the problems didn't go away. Wednesday night's performance still contained goofs and **Dick Berger** was fighting mad. On Thursday morning he called his lighting director, **Lloyd Evans,** into his office. He paced the floor, hoisted up the waistband of his pants, turned and stared at his light man, and roared three little words—"Lloyd, it's Thursday."

★ For the opening night of Starlight's first show, *The Desert Song*, the composer, **Sigmund Romberg**, was invited to conduct the overture. For his efforts he was given a commemorative plaque that read "*The Dessert Song* 1951."

★ Before one night's performance of *Annie Get Your Gun* in 1953, **Janis Paige** fell ill. **Dick Berger** went to the understudy and discovered she had not learned the part well enough to give a performance. Berger refused to concede defeat and send the audience home. Instead he decided to play the part of Annie himself. He read the lines and walked through the blocking, the understudy sang the songs, and the audience had a unique theatre experience. (He never tried to play a lead female role again!)

★ **Joe Macaulay**, the character actor seen for many years on the Starlight stage, once was arrested for fencing with a tree. The arresting officer did not believe his story about practicing for a duel scene in an upcoming play, and **Dick Berger** had to rescue Joe from the jail cell. This incident happened in St. Louis, years before these two would meet again at Starlight. Needless to say, when Macaulay came to the Kansas City theatre, he avoided dueling with the pin oaks in Swope Park.

★ The same **Joe Macaulay** used to apply his character makeup with a towel draped over his head. He was not about to give away trade secrets.

★ **Ginger Rogers** came to Starlight in 1964 to perform the lead role in *Tovarich*. She brought with her an expensive wardrobe and the vaudeville custom that she be paid in cash before each performance. She also brought with her a taste for the genuine—diamonds, not rhinestones, darling! At the end of the play, when the lead character was reunited with the aristocracy and a crown placed on her head, Ginger insisted that the crown, necklace, and earrings all be real diamonds, not the imitation type. She and

50

Dick Berger had numerous disagreements over this issue. On dress rehearsal night, when the crown of rhinestones was presented to her, she picked up the tiara and broke it in half. She looked out in the audience area at Berger and said, "Oh—I broke it." Berger knew he was up against a stone wall, so opening night Ginger sported real gems (rented from Tivol's) on her head.

★ Before **Dick Berger** became the producing director of Starlight in 1951, he had New York experience ranging from ticket boy, proofreader, casting director, and producer. He discovered some new talent in New York as well as at Starlight Theatre. Many of these young men and women went on to take their place in the entertainment world. One of Berger's favorite stories involved his experience as a play reader for a director of a Broadway show. His job was to find a black girl who matched the physical appearance of the leading white girl in the show *Dance with Your Gods*. During the play's voodoo scene, the identities of the two girls switched back and forth. Berger went looking through the clubs in Harlem to find just the right tall beautiful girl. He found what he thought was the perfect lady. After her show, he spoke with her about appearing in a Broadway play. She was most receptive to the idea but warned that he would have to talk with her father, who picked her up every night from the theatre. Berger stayed that night and chatted with the parent who gave an OK to the idea.

PHOTO COURTESY OF STARLIGHT THEATRE

Ginger Rogers, *Tovarich*, 1964.

The next Monday she arrived as scheduled at Dick's theatre. Though she only had a few lines of dialogue, she was working out nicely. A week later, however, she failed to appear for rehearsal. The director promptly informed Berger that he was to go check out the reason for her absence. He went back to the Harlem club but was escorted out the back door by a bouncer twice his size who growled, "Don't return to get the girl. She's not going to work for Broadway or for any other place. She's working only for this club!" Berger returned to his director with the bad news. The director informed Berger that the girl was to report for work the next Monday "no matter what." Berger, being of sound mind but small body, hired a few "intimidating friends" to go and "reason" with the bouncer. The next Monday the girl appeared at rehearsal, and the career of **Lena Horne** was launched.

★ Pirates were needed for the 1959 operetta *The New Moon*. A huge crowd of strong, vicious-looking men was required for the pirate invasion scene, and there simply weren't enough chorus men to do the scene well. Why not take the **Stage Crew** and augment the cast? Why not? The offstage restrooms were converted into dressing rooms for "the stars," and every night after the crew had finished the scene right before the pirate act, they went into the "dressing rooms" and costumed themselves in the outrageous attire they had brought from home or borrowed for the occasion. They came crawling over the side of the ship, some even wearing eye patches, brandishing the carefully sculpted knives and swords they had made. They enacted the subsequent fight scene with vigor, much to the delight of the audience as well as **Phil de Rosier**,

The New Moon, 1959. Rick Berger, who later became president of Walt Disney Productions and Metro Goldwyn Mayer/United Artists is second from the left.

who was fortunate enough to be watching from the wings. The future president of Metro Goldwyn Mayer/United Artists, **Rick Berger**, was one of those hearty mates.

★ When **Dick Berger** asked **Ancel Lacy**, the master carpenter, to find work for son Rick to do backstage, he did so with reluctance. The father didn't want anyone coming to him and saying that his son was lazy or inefficient. Son Richard, in his zeal to please his father, did cause a problem. Lacy came in one day to see Berger and pleaded, "Will you please tell Rick not to be too eager to lift that heavy lumber? It seems that when he does it so quickly, all the weight goes to the other end."

★ When **Dick Berger** first came to Kansas City to audition talent for the theatre's upcoming season, he spent a long afternoon in the center of the auditorium at the Kansas City Art Institute. He had not thought he would find too many possibilities, but at the end of the afternoon he had discovered five singers with outstanding voices. When he learned that they had all studied with the same teacher, **Harold A. Decker**, at Wichita, Kansas University, Berger placed a call to the teacher, had him come to town, and signed him as the associate musical director. Moral: Good students make good advertising for teachers.

★ Opening night in 1951 was dazzling for the audience but frantic for the production staff, who had to be certain that all would go well. **Roland Fiore**, the music director, had forgotten his black tuxedo pants, and the French legionnaire costume on hand backstage offered unsuitable trousers for a white tuxedo jacket. **Jim McQueeny**, the publicity director for Starlight, dashed home, retrieved his own dressy pants, and gave them to Roland, who wore them in those opening moments of *The Desert Song* overture. The problem was that Roland wore those same pants for the overture of every show for the next several seasons. Jim never again was the proud wearer of those trousers. They are now a part of Starlight's history.

★ **Biff McGuire**, one of the principals in *Roberta* (1951), called the business office early one Sunday morning saying that he wanted to be paid in cash that evening as he was scheduled to fly to London early the next day and couldn't negotiate a check there. So he was paid with multiple small bills from the box office cash before the performance. He held onto those bills throughout the earlier scenes, but when the time came for him to enter for his big number, he turned to the fellow next to him whom he took to be a stagehand and said, "Hold this d— roll for me 'til I get back." He handed the man the wad of bills and went out into the spotlights. When he returned, the man was still there—fortunately. It seems that the man was not a stagehand at all but a theatre patron who had accidentally wandered backstage in search of the restrooms.

★ When **Carol Burnett** came to town for her role in *Calamity Jane* in 1961, she proved to be the warm human being she portrays on the television screen. She would sometimes hang around the theatre during her off hours. Several times she took over the switchboard and answered calls while the regular operator was having dinner in the backstage cafe. If the caller would inquire about the *Calamity Jane* show, Carol would give all the necessary information along with the comment, "You'll love that Carol Burnett—-she's the greatest." Never did the caller know that she had been talking with Calamity Jane herself.

★ The singers at Starlight did not make much money for all their work. **Cara Ann Wilcox** and **Pam Miller**, ensemble members during the hot and humid summer of 1967, decided to add to their meager earnings by placing a ten-foot wading pool near the singers' pavilion and charging twenty-five cents for admission. Ah but did they report their extra earnings to the IRS?

★ Sometimes talent for the stage is measured in some peculiar ways. During the 1952 season, stage director **Edward Reveaux** was auditioning members of the singing ensemble for a bit part that required a young lady to scream as two young men chased her across the stage. The screaming reached such a frenzy that the park police came to investigate. Top honors went to **Betty Jean Worrel**.

★ **Dean Ryan**, the associate musical director from 1960-68 and the resident musical director from 1969-71, was extra poor his first season at Starlight. **Al Krikorian**, the prop man, introduced him to poker. Ryan bought a book that explained all the different hands, plus their value and probability, and he carefully studied this text. He was ready! Thursday night after the Starlight show a group would gather and play cards until the wee hours of the morning. The first week Dean brought $50 worth of quarters. He lost them all. He went home and delved further into the poker book. The next week he brought $50 worth of quarters. He lost again. The third week he read, re-read, and read again that book in hopes that his luck would change. He went to the poker party and again lost all his money. That early morning when he returned home, he walked over to his treasured book and calmly dropped it in the wastebasket. Directing the orchestra for **Dick Berger** paid higher dividends than betting against those Starlight stagehands.

★ During one of the 1962 performances of *Around the World in Eighty Days*, one of the male dancers exhibited remarkable ingenuity. During the ship-burning scene, when the principal characters are trying to dash home, make their deadline, and win their bet, the boards for the boat had been assembled so that they would tear off easily and fall inside the ship. One of the chorus people got a little carried away with the scene and proceeded to rip a board off and throw it out onto the stage. One of the dancers, recognizing the hazards of leaving this board on stage for the next scene, proceeded to jump off the ship,

Calamity Jane, 1961. Richard Berger, Carol Burnett, and Maurice Breyer (Starlight Association President).

belly swim on the hard Starlight stage over to the plank, rescue the missing board, and belly swim back to the ship.

★ In that same production, **Jan McArt**, the leading lady, was to be carried up the stairway to the top of a burning pyre. The whole pyre scene was built on a rolling platform, and around the bottom was an asbestos cloth soaked in kerosene. When she passed by the cloth area, the stagehand in the back of the platform was supposed to light the cloth and flames would quickly engulf the bottom section of the pyre. One night the winds were exceptionally high. As Jan passed by the cloth and the stagehand lit the fire, her long flowing dress was caught by the breeze and floated into the fire. The curtain quickly closed. Fortunately, Jan was not hurt. She was, however, plenty frightened by that sequence of events, so the next day considerable time was spent timing the cue for that scene.

★ While leading ladies were catching fire, the male leads of that show were having their problems too. For the balloon scene, a huge crane was assembled to lift the balloon and basket up over the orchestra pit area. The two men were in the basket joyfully singing about their adventures and drinking champagne. Trouble was, one of the men was airsick every night, and as he bent down in the basket, supposedly to get glasses and more champagne, he actually was vomiting in a bucket provided for such purpose.

★ *Around the World in Eighty Days* spawned many a headache. During one of the performances, the ostrich decided to park in the middle of the stage. The trainer, who was dressed as a desert person, pulled and tugged and coaxed but to no avail. **Roland Fiore** was madly creating extra bars of music down in the orchestra pit to cover this unforeseen delay in the action. When the ostrich finally decided to move on, audience and crew rolled with laughter when they saw the giant egg the bird had deposited center stage.

★ Not all the romances of Starlight were portrayed on stage. When **Gordon and Sheila MacRae** were headlining *Annie Get Your Gun* in 1960, their daughter, **Meredith**, met a handsome stagehand. Seems they had a lot in common—show business parents, a love for the theatre, and much more. Meredith later married the stagehand whose name was **Richard Berger**, the son of the producer at Starlight.

★ In the 1965 production of *Camelot*, a big parade was to open the show. Actors were in place, the orchestra was set, but the lights went out—all the lights. Rather than lose the audience, **Dick Berger** brought out the cast individually to sing and entertain the audience. The performers were lit by flashlight until the proper lighting was reinstated. It seems that a snake had crawled into the transformer, shorting everything out.

★ More on animals. During one hot muggy July night's performance, a family of skunks invaded the backstage area. When the giant act curtain closed, one of these visitors was accidentally killed. His unbearable "fragrance" lingered throughout the

PHOTOS COURTESY OF STARLIGHT THEATRE

Above: **Jan McArt,** leading lady in *Around the World in Eighty Days,* 1962.

Below: **Gordon and Sheila MacRae** with staging director Bert Yarborough. *The Bells are Ringing,* 1959.

THE STORY OF STARLIGHT THEATRE

entire performance to the utter dismay of cast and crew.

★ Award for the best spontaneous comic remark must go to **Steve Allen**, a master of the clever quip. During one evening's performance in 1974, Steve was on stage along with the orchestra, which was located there for this show. He held a microphone in his hand and began to walk toward the audience. A narrow, four-foot wide plank had been built over the empty Starlight orchestra pit, connecting the stage area to a horizontal runway in front of the first row of seats. Even though the edges of the plank were lit, Steve misjudged the distance and tumbled into the orchestra pit—a seven-foot drop onto cement. After he was seen falling into the pit, the audience heard him remarking, "Well, I fell into the orchestra pit. (Pause). I've never done that before! (Longer pause.) Somebody bring me a ladder." He was retrieved from the pit unscathed and finished the show with all of his natural good humor intact.

PHOTO COURTESY OF STARLIGHT THEATRE

Gordon and Sheila MacRae in *Annie Get Your Gun*, 1960.

★ The stagehand who traveled with the 1967 production of *It's a Bird, It's a Plane, It's Superman* liked to indulge. So much so that on several nights he didn't get the proper amount of counterweight in place and smashed Superman into the side of the pylons. Up, up, and away!

★ During the same show, Superman, to prove his superior force, labored and struggled to get a tall lamp stand bent into horseshoe shape. Then, with as much muscle and effort, he bent the tall lamp stem back into its original straight shape. When he finished his mighty feat, he placed the lamp stand across his knees. One night something didn't click or fasten, and the lamp stand proceeded to droop to the stage floor all by itself much to the amusement of the audience and the crew.

★ Feminists beware! **Harding Dorn**, the resident choreographer at Starlight for years, once got into an argument with one of the female singers. He wanted her to move around the stage in a particularly graceful manner that proved too complicated for her. The young woman complained, "I'm not a dancer—I'm a singer!" Dorn replied, "You're not a singer—you're a dumb broad!" The young woman proceeded to file a complaint with the theatre management. **Dick Berger** brought a close friend of Dorn's into his office, sat him down, and pleaded, "You've got to tell Harding that he can't call these dumb broads 'dumb broads.' He's got to call them 'beautiful.'"

★ At the end of each season, the dancing ensemble would honor one of its members

PHOTO COURTESY OF JERRY FUNK

Superman with producer Dick Berger in *It's a Bird, It's a Plane, It's Superman*, 1967.

PHOTO COURTESY OF STARLIGHT THEATRE

Richard Berger with the cast of *Li'l Abner*, 1959.

for his or her numerous goofs throughout the season. **Harding Dorn** received the "Betty Fudge Award" in 1969 for his unusual disappearing act. He was walking out in the audience area during a daytime rehearsal, megaphone in hand, barking orders to his dancers on stage, when he suddenly disappeared. His whole body just simply went away. It seems that every day during the summer, large fire hoses were used on the audience area to clean the seats for the evening's performance. The large drains in front of the orchestra area were left open so that the water could flow down the audience slope and into the drains. Any doubt where Dorn had gone?

★ **George Wasko**, assistant to the staging director in 1963 and an actor on the Starlight stage for many years, had short but tart advice for young actors on the huge Starlight stage: "Don't try to act! Just say the line and get off the stage."

★ **Dick Berger** had a dance number in his head for years. The dance was never performed at Starlight, though he threatened to practice it on more than a few occasions. Anytime there was a problem with the union about treatment of its dancers or singers, the complaint would always be lodged with Berger. He periodically would call in his staff and state, "OK, if we have to play by the rules, so do they. Make the dancers do the walking number." When questioned by one of the newer staff members as to what the "walking number" was, Berger told him, "Union rules require the dancers to work for six hours. If you don't have anything specific for them to do, put them in a big circle and have them walk around. We don't know when we're going to use that number, but they'll have to practice it anyway."

★ It was not uncommon for the crew to play tricks on the cast on the closing night of a show. In the 1959 production of *Li'l Abner*, when several performers jumped into a barrel at the end of their dance number, the unsuspecting dancers found that the barrel had been lined with limburger cheese. Whoops!

★ In the 1970 production of *How to Succeed in Business Without Really Trying*, the lead character, **Robert Morse**, had a scene in which he talked on a telephone. The prop phone was "dead," and the actor had only himself to listen to. However, Morse, known for his practical jokes (such as going out during intermission and selling popcorn in the audience area), got the tables turned on him one evening. The sound crew hooked up the telephone. When Morse lifted the receiver to his ear, he got the voice of **Michael Bradshaw**, the stage manager. Only those two know for sure what was said, but from the look on Morse's face, it must have been some pretty spicy patter.

★ **Buster West**, who played Benjamin Kidd in the 1951 production *The Desert Song*, the year of the great Kansas City flood, stood under his umbrella and pronounced, "This is the wettest—desert I have ever been in."

★ On the less humorous side, **Jim Hawthorne** began singing "Oh What a Beautiful Morning" at the beginning of *Oklahoma!* in 1954. When he had finished the song and was standing on the leading lady's porch to begin the dialogue, he fell over backwards. The large act curtain closed in order to shield the eyes of the audience from this mishap. In a short while, the curtain opened and the play resumed. No one in the audience knew that the World War II veteran had a steel plate in his head, which occasionally caused him to black out.

★ Now hear this! **Milton Berle** was starring in the show *Two by Two* during 1971. He was the only character to have a wireless microphone on him, which, of course, made his every word much more audible than the other players. He was constantly concerning himself with his volume, even to the extent of phoning the sound man at home. He proclaimed, "I want to be ten times louder than everybody else, so when I twitch my ear, you bring the volume up." During one of his performances, he even went so far as to sing a few words of his song and then say "Put it up, Ray," right in the middle of the lyrics.

★ Mutiny! **Roland Fiore** often quickened the tempo of songs and dances, which totally provoked the unsuspecting singers and dancers. One evening, during the 1965 performance of *110 in the Shade*, the dancers turned the tables. **George Church** was a professional dancer who had been in the original Broadway company of *Oklahoma!* and had created the role on Broadway of the character he was portraying at Starlight. In one scene he sat on the stage and opened a picnic basket. Out came an imaginary person whose sounds were made by the drummer in the orchestra. The dancers on stage clapped the echo of the beat of the drummer and George began to dance in rhythm. When Roland raised his baton to start the orchestra, he increased the tempo significantly, and the dancers knew that George would have a very difficult time keeping up with the musicians. They decided that enough was enough—Roland was going to have to be reasonable or look silly. So

PHOTO COURTESY OF STARLIGHT THEATRE

South Pacific, 1957. *Left to right:*
Jim Hawthorne, Joe Macaulay,
George S. Irving, Benny Baker.

while Roland had the musicians playing the bars of music allegro, the dancers continued to clap the original rhythm. Finally, Roland had to relent or ruin the scene. He stopped the orchestra, and began again. This time he marched to the beat of the dancers' "drum."

★ During one of the productions of *Fiddler on the Roof* (we won't say which one), a certain male chorus member was not particularly liked by the stage crew, who decided to play a little joke on him. The man was supposed to carry a chicken cage onto the stage. The crew built a false bottom in the cage. The first night they left the compartment empty. The next night they put in a five-pound weight. The next evening they added another weight, and so on until by the end of the week that chorus member was nearly dragging himself and the chicken cage across the huge Starlight stage. He never caught on.

★ In a scene from *Annie Get Your Gun* when Annie and Frank Butler are having their clay pigeon shoot-out, the sequence of events was supposed to have gone like this: one character says "Pull," aims the rifle, pulls the trigger, and Buffalo Bill shouts "Hit!" Annie and Frank battle this one out multiple times with the "Pull" "Hit" dialogue continuing. Once, though, the rifle misfired. There was no sound of a gun going off, but Buffalo Bill shouted "Hit" anyway. The actors looked at each other and the audience, and everyone had a good laugh that was not written into the script.

★ During the 1950s and '60s when Starlight still used the carbon arc type spotlights, those lamps had to be tested occasionally. On one warm summer evening, a spotlight operator focused his light on the grassy hill that used to be behind the Starlight stage. He found he had lit a threesome who were not reading Shakespeare under the stars. He called to his fellow operators, "Scooby Doo on the hillside" and all four huge spotlights focused on three very embarrassed people who quickly grabbed their clothes and made for the bushes.

★ Van's, The Swope Park Bar, The Tavern on the Green—all were names of the same popular hangout for the ensemble groups during the 1950s and '60s. Located on the corner of Sixty-seventh and Cleveland, the cook served huge sandwiches, the owner loved the show-people clientele, and it was the only air-conditioned building everyone could fit into. Many former Starlight performers have fond memories of the place.

★ Being the producing director at Starlight was always a demanding job, but sometimes *really* important matters vied for his attention. One summer afternoon **Dick Berger** got a call from a little girl, **Carol Vannaman**, who lived in his neighborhood. She complained to him that his son **Rick**, and two other neighborhood boys (her brother, **John Vannaman**, and young **Bob Menesse**) had shot BB holes in all the cups she had planned on using to sell her lemonade at the street corner. Berger immediately left the theatre, drove straight home, took his son into the house, and gave him a spanking. That was the last raid on little Carol's lemonade stand by the pesky "Three

Musketeers." Starlight had lost its producer for an hour, but free enterprise was saved at Janssen Place!

★ The 1965 season was known to the ensemble group as the "Salamenchee Summer." The name was derived from a misunderstanding of one of the opening show's songs. *Camelot* headed the season that year. During the execution scene, the dancers were on stage, wearing hooded gear and carrying torches, while the singers were in the tunnels. The chorus was loudly proclaiming, "Saw the men she held most dear go to war for Guinevere." The dancers, who were quite far away from the chorus and hooded besides, never could unscramble those words. They began to greet each other with the salutation "Salamenchee" in mimic of the words "Saw the men she." The greeting was good-naturedly continued throughout the season.

★ Some of the kids who lived near the large Swope Park theatre had their own ideas of how to celebrate the Fourth of July. A group of them would sneak up next to the backstage fence and toss firecrackers over the top in order to create a disturbance. **Dr. Joseph Spalitto**, a Kansas City dentist, confessed to being one of those hooligans.

★ Be careful what you wish for! Sometimes your dreams come true, as was the case for Dr. Spalitto's mother. During the 1957 season her son was a friend of the young boy whose parents were the caretakers at the theatre. The two chums would idle away many hours behind the scenes and in the backstage cafeteria. **Tony Bennett** was starring in *Silk Stockings* that year. One day Mrs. Spalitto remarked to her son offhandedly that she would like to feed that great entertainer some real pizza for a change. The next day while her son was walking backstage he encountered the performer and asked him over for a genuine Italian feast. Bennett accepted. Mrs. Spalitto was flabbergasted when her son informed her that she was hosting "the man who left his heart in San Francisco" for dinner.

★ **Dick Berger** sometimes had some rather unorthodox ways of auditioning folks. During one particular session, he had waited in an auditorium with his friend, **Joe Hall**, for a certain fellow to show up. When the man failed to appear, Berger and Hall got up to leave. The man came scurrying through the door and shook Berger's hand, apologizing for his tardiness. Berger spoke to him for a minute or so, hired him on the spot without hearing him sing, and left the auditorium. As they were walking away, Hall asked why he had hired a man whom he didn't even know could sing a note. Berger replied, "I shook his hand. It was clammy, so I knew he needed the job. After I listened to him explain what he had already done in the theatre, I knew he'd work out."

★ **Victoria Sherry**, leading female performer in 1952's *East Wind*, remembers trying to sing melodious love songs with after-the-rain grasshoppers crawling all over the front of her veil.

PHOTO COURTESY OF STARLIGHT THEATRE

Julie Wilson and Tony Bennett in *Silk Stockings*, 1957.

The Artists and Technicians

Professional performances require more than just a nice facility and a strong director. Theatre is a collaborative effort. A great production is the result of more than just the appearance of a "star" who sings a glorious melody, shares a sparkling wit, or gracefully bounds across the stage. A superior show represents a crystallization of a variety of skills focused on a single goal—perfection of the performance moment. If the theatre patrons could not see the sets and the actors adequately, they would be unhappy. If they could not hear the music and the dialogue, plays would be dull indeed. If *The Music Man*'s Professor Harold Hill would come marching down River City's Main Street in an unsuitable costume, the patrons would not believe. If the giant Starlight sets were not authentic to the period, as well as large enough to be seen and designed well enough to keep the actor in proper perspective, the viewing public would be uneasy, uncomfortable, and probably unreturning. Effective props, a well-played musical score, and appropriate dances well executed all comprise aspects of a production that don't just emerge on opening night. In addition to those elements that are noticed by the theatre patrons, there are multiple aspects of a performance that are never seen by the paying public. Jerry Funk, a former Starlight stage manager, wrote in the *Independence Pictorial News:*

It is the stagehands who operate the curtain, run the spotlights, tie down the units so wind can't shift them around, set and plug in the microphones, run electrical cable from the power source to lights on the units, fire the offstage gun shots, do emergency repairs on backstage equipment and literally hundreds of other jobs, all of which are as necessary to a smooth production as an actor's performance.

PORGY AND BESS • THE SOUND OF MUSIC • CAMELOT • HERE'S LOVE • 110 IN THE SHADE • SHE LOVES ME • OLIVER! • HOW TO SUCCEED IN BUSINESS WITHOUT REALLY TRYING • ON A CLEAR DAY YOU CAN SEE FOREVER • FUNNY GIRL • IT'S A BIRD! IT'S A PLANE! IT'S SUPERMAN! •SWEET CHARITY • STATE FAIR • GEORGE M! • MAME • HELLO, DOLLY! • MAN OF LA MANCHA • FIDDLER ON THE ROOF • 70 GIRLS 70 • CABARET • TWO BY TWO • GONE WITH THE WIND • ON THE TOWN • 1776 • SHENANDOAH •

Left: **Harding Dorn** and the Starlight Dance Ensemble. Dancers listed on page 62.

Dancers as shown on page 60:
First row, left to right: Karen Lorhan, Judith McAvoy, Odelia Aguilera, Harding Dorn (choreographer), Suanne Jackson, Kay Kelly, Denee Jaggers.
Second row, left to right: Leanne Arnfield, Vicki Allen, Kathy Bartosh, Mimi Wathen, Sandahl Bergman, Cheryl Clark.
Third row, left to right: Robert Page Priko, Ron Sukiennik, Dennis Landsman, Kendall Dingman, Jr., Paul Stevens and Scott Barnard.

The unusual problems of each of the ten aspects of backstage work (set design, scenic artistry, musical direction, choreography, stage managing, carpentry, properties, costumes, sound, and lights) are compounded by the immense size of Starlight. The story of the artists and technicians who had to overcome those difficulties is a tale of devotion, talent, and persistence. Each person, who served as head of a particular department for the longest time throughout the four decades plus of the theatre's existence, has a special niche in Starlight's history. It is those backstage personnel who are truly the unsung "stars" of Starlight.

SET DESIGNER

G. PHILIPPE DE ROSIER

The fortunate ones are those who really know what they want to do with their life. If you can do what you've always wanted to, you'll be happy and fulfilled. I hooked my wagon to a star a long time ago, and it's been a tremendous ride.

Phil de Rosier (1987 interview) with Dory de Angelo for *K.C. Life Downtown* magazine)

"A stage designer is an accompanist. You have to tune yourself to a book or a show or a star. If you (the viewer) go home humming the scenery, you've seen a bad show," remarked Phil de Rosier in 1972 to Brenda Fisher, a *Kansas City Times* reporter. But many a person left Starlight marveling at the lush sets that had enhanced the show they had just experienced. Phil de Rosier designed over two hundred productions during his Starlight career. The sets for the 1950s, '60s and first half of the '70s bore the mark of his distinctive artistic style.

De Rosier was a staff designer for NBC and CBS when someone mentioned his name to Richard Berger as a possible candidate for the Starlight job. Berger was looking for someone who knew how to design for a large outdoor theatre, and de Rosier had worked at the Tanglewood Opera Festival, the summer home of the Boston Symphonic Orchestra. Several schools were attached to the festival—a school of opera, a school of instrumental music, and a school of voice. Leonard Bernstein and Leontyne Price also were working at the festival when de Rosier was designing sixty-foot high scenery for the productions.

He made an appointment with Berger in his New York office. "The second I met him, I liked him," reported de Rosier thirty-eight years later. "He took me to lunch and offered me the job." De Rosier was particularly pleased with the offer because, as he had left Berger's office, he had spied the name of his competitor on Berger's calendar as the next appointment. Evidently that engagement was never kept.

When de Rosier came to Kansas City to inspect the theatre, he felt welcome. He was met by Mayor John B. Gage and taken to the Muehlebach Hotel for lunch with

other Starlight board members. That feeling of specialness and regard for his mission at Starlight never left de Rosier, even after four decades.

In his first years at Starlight, he split his time between Kansas City in the spring and summer months, and New York for the autumn and winter seasons. The pressure of those jobs was horrendous. When a designer left New York for such a long period of time, he lost his touch and his connections. After two seasons of this split shift, de Rosier went to New Mexico and bought a little hacienda in a town with a population of 1. The quiet and the beauty of the place did wonderful things to his spirit. Berger was concerned, though, that he might lose his designer, so he phoned and asked de Rosier if he could come and talk with him. The conversation went as follows:

"I'll fly to New Mexico. I'll fly out to Albuquerque," Berger suggested.

"I'll come pick you up at the airport," de Rosier countered.

"Don't bother, I'll take a cab," replied Berger, the proverbial New Yorker.

With a note of urgency in his voice, de Rosier replied, "But Dick, it's three hundred miles."

De Rosier drove the distance, met Berger, and took him back to the beauty of the fruit trees that surrounded his home. They talked. They agreed that with a little creative budgeting, Starlight could afford to pay de Rosier what he needed to survive in New Mexico if he would devote his entire energies to the Kansas City project. The

Production staff, 1956. *Left to right: (front row seated)* Roland Fiore, musical director; Richard Berger, producing director; Glenn Jordan, staging director; *(back row standing)* Jack Lee, associate musical director; Anthony Ferrara, stage manager; Walter Swift, assistant to stage director; James Jamieson, choreographer; G. Philippe de Rosier, scenic designer; Donn Murphy, lighting director; Charles Murawski, assistant stage manager; and Harding Dorn, ensemble staging director.

The Artists and Technicians

deal was made. Phil de Rosier became the resident Starlight designer and continued for twenty-four years until 1975, when he did not renew his yearly contract. Oftentimes he also designed for other Kansas City groups. He was the first designer for The Renaissance Festival, and occasionally designed for the Kansas City Lyric Opera, the Missouri Repertory, and for conventions and flower shows around the town. However, his main source of income and attention was the great theatre in Swope Park.

De Rosier had unique problems to overcome at Starlight. The stage spans twice the width of those on Broadway, the scenery looms two stories high, and the audience area is at least tenfold that of the New York houses. All that translated to size, spectacle, and proper perspective. What appeared lavish to the spectators in the orchestra section had to appear gorgeous to those who were nearly three hundred feet away in the back row. What appeared casual and in keeping with room size from the vantage point of the box seats had to be visible to the audience members seated at the base of the light towers. It was a tough assignment. The wide range of productions, from light opera to musical comedy to variety shows with single-set backdrops, provided multiple opportunities for his imaginative prowess. Such variety also set up pitfalls for any designer who was not constantly creating and rearranging his thoughts. Just the scope of the project was sometimes overwhelming. There was enough paint used on Starlight scenery to repaint the entire length of Ward Parkway several times, enough lumber and nails during the season to build four large houses, and enough light in a single show to light up all of Swope Park. That kind of bigness required an expert designer.

Son of an auto mechanic and a homemaker, Phil de Rosier seemed born to create for the theatre—he made his first miniature stage set at age five. His career began as a high school art teacher. A graduate in architecture at the Massachusetts College of Art, he earned a Master of Arts degree from work at Vanderbilt University and the Yale School of Design. He served in World War II in Europe in counterintelligence work, and then spent a year in Paris and Rome studying lighting, costuming, and setting techniques. "Architecture was the best possible background for scenic designing at Starlight," de Rosier once explained. "You can't learn this in school. It takes a specialist to envision twenty-foot scenery."

Work started in December for the new season, with each show requiring about a month to complete scenery design. If it was a book show, de Rosier first would acquaint himself with the script and make thumbnail sketches. Then he would map out diagrams of the stage and its components to guide the carpenters in their work. He also created cardboard models and detailed paintings of the sets. When show time neared, he would provide the list of all props needed. He also designed all the lighting for Starlight shows. Saturday nights and early Sunday mornings were spent watching the dress rehearsal and marking the cues for the lighting technicians to note.

Back in the early 1950s wonderful things could be accomplished for as little as $40,000—a price that included cast, union help, and materials. Times have changed.

G. Philippe de Rosier, scenic designer.

By comparison, $40,000 in the 1992 season would fall slightly short of the cost of 1482 tickets in the orchestra section.

De Rosier was an overall person of the theatre. He could paint a set, stitch a costume, discard a prop as inappropriate, mix and match a wardrobe for a character in a period show, or simply appreciate songs and dances elegantly performed as he watched from the Starlight wings. He knew it all.

Phil de Rosier died in March of 1991. A resident of Santa Fe at the time, he made frequent return trips to visit Kansas City, the town he loved. A memorial service was held in his honor at Starlight in the most fitting of surroundings—the paint shop. A gathering of family and friends filled the corrugated open-aired structure, which was almost church-like in its atmosphere. Flats had been masked and greenery put in place around the interior. A Roman arch, a survivor of some former production, was suspended from the roof. Its shape conflicted yet complemented the angled ceiling beams of the simple building that de Rosier had presided over for twenty-four years. The great designer would have felt right at home.

The Artists and Technicians

ROLAND FIORE

His first appearance at Starlight was quite formal. Dressed in Jim McQueeny's tuxedo (see the intermission section), Roland Fiore walked out into the Kansas City night with a spotlight beaming on him. He accepted the conductor's baton from his friend, Sigmund Romberg, and began an eighteen-year career as Starlight's maestro. In later years, he was known to conduct the orchestra wearing a tuxedo jacket over a pair of shorts (which were never seen by the audience). But in those first years of the theatre's existence, proper attire as well as proper attention to musical integrity were the order of the day.

Dick Berger had listened to the strains of the orchestra at the Memphis Open Air Theatre and had liked what he heard. He contacted the conductor's agent, Henry Wiese, and hired Fiore for the Starlight maestro's position. It was a position which, in Fiore's own words forty years later, proved to be "a fabulous experience. The people of Kansas City were wonderful. We had a great theatre, a great producer, and great artists."

Fiore came to Kansas City with a wealth of musical credits. Born in America but reared in Italy, he had been the organist at the age of fifteen at John's Street Methodist Church in New York. He studied with Vidittorio Giannini and Tibor Serlyn as well as under the tutelage of the French Opera Wing at the Metropolitan Opera. He had been associated with the New York Center Opera company and Berkshire Music Festival, had been a musical director for the Shuberts in New York, and had conducted chamber symphony concerts at Carnegie Hall and for Voice of America broadcasts.

Fiore also had a beautiful and talented wife, Victoria Sherry, who came to the Kansas City theatre with him. Miss Sherry sang the lead in Starlight's first show as well as succeeding productions of *The Vagabond King, East Wind, The New Moon, The Three Musketeers,* and *Cole Porter Festival.* She is now the producer of the Piccola Opera of Philadelphia, for which Fiore acts as conductor.

One of his first major jobs as a conductor came as a result of his wife's soprano virtuosity. Sherry auditioned for the New York Opera and was offered a touring position in a Gilbert and Sullivan comic opera (which she hated). Someone suggested that her voice might be better suited to a touring job opening up with the Shubert organization. She auditioned for them and was hired as the leading lady of *Blossom Time.* The producers soon learned she was in love with a young conductor who wanted to be with her, so the Shubert team offered Fiore the conducting job for the touring company. Together the two high school sweethearts from Jersey City traveled across the country performing. Sherry later sang with the Romberg company. When Berger decided to produce *The Desert Song* as his first offering at Starlight, he invited the composer to the Midwest theatre with a promise that one of Romberg's own singers would be playing the lead and another of his friends would be conducting the orchestra.

Roland Fiore at piano. Singers *(left to right)* Barbara Priest, Patsy Peterson, Pat Marling, Carolyn Sager, Rosemary Harrell Jackson, Barbara Bernandy, Patty Byler, Thelma Foxworthy, Joan Fagan and Kathryn Henry.

The first seasons at Starlight set the stage for the later years when the outdoor theatre came to be regarded as one of the finest in the country. The style of the productions was always genuine. That is, Berger and Fiore both agreed that the music should be played as it was written; the style was never to be tampered with, interpreted, or modernized in any way. "Do it with esprit but do it as the composer intended" was their motto. Fiore was generally familiar with the popular scores, but if any questions arose as to intent or execution, he would sometimes visit with the composer to get his opinion. Romberg and Friml were both consulted on scores for the Starlight audiences.

To find the voices suited to singing the lead parts for the early operettas, Fiore sometimes accompanied Berger to Steinway Hall near Fifty-seventh Street in New York to hear Starlight hopefuls. Although he never attended the auditions held locally, he expected New York quality in all singers on the Starlight stage. As he coached the singing ensemble, he often pushed the singers to project their voices with strength and richness. He sometimes would complain, "You don't have enough 'pancake' in your sound." His prodding earned him the nickname "Rolling Fury" by the ensemble. Fiore's criticisms, however, were not restricted to the singing ensemble. Often he would rankle the orchestra with comments like "You're crumbling" or "You're failing me miserably." All knew why he was demanding more from their performances. They tried to oblige.

The Artists and Technicians   67

Roland Fiore with Dean Ryan
seated at the piano.

"Kansas City musicians were first class," reported Fiore. During the 1950s and '60s, thirty-six members of the Starlight orchestra came from the ranks of the Kansas City Philharmonic Orchestra. Many were delighted to be a part of Starlight during the summer months. According to Frank Franano, the present personnel manager of the Kansas City Symphony Orchestra, the experience was not just the satisfaction of a job. It was devotion to the company, a chance to be part of the theatre and contribute to it. Sometimes those contributions were hazardous to one's health. When the rains would come, the oboe player would be the first to leave. Soon after, the flutists and the woodwinds would follow. The string musicians would grab their second instruments to play in the dampness. When the droplets became too frequent and too heavy, all but the pianist and a few brass would head for protection under the stage, leaving Fiore and a few rain-soaked companions to carry the weight of the musical portion of the show.

The Kansas City musicians had to be very professional in order to keep up with the demands of their work at Starlight. Saturday afternoons on the singers' pavilion presented the first opportunity to play the score with other members of the orchestra. On Sunday afternoons the musicians again gathered on the singers' pavilion, away from the blazing hot sun, to practice with the principals for the next week's show. It was not until opening night on Monday that the entire score was played without interruption. The musicians performed every night of the week plus the additional weekend afternoon rehearsals. There was no time for inexperience or ineptitude.

When Fiore decided to leave Starlight in the late 1960s, he did so with a twinge of regret. A change was coming about, brought on by accessibility of television and the advent of home air conditioning, and increasingly aggravated by the city's acquisition in 1955 of a professional baseball team whose games were played mostly at night. Attendance was dropping at the theatre, not because the productions were not excellent, but because it was more comfortable to stay at home on hot summer nights. In addition, Fiore had built a beautiful home in New Hope, Pennsylvania, and wanted to spend more of his time there. The 1968 season was his last with Starlight. Remembering his departure, Fiore said, "The experience had been so complete—an incredibly close warm personal feeling—what more could we have asked for in life?"

Fiore was the only member of the Starlight production staff, Berger included, who had any time off during the season. As Sunday evening was his designated night away, his assistant took over the directing responsibilities. Dean Ryan was the associate musical director from 1960 until 1968. His job responsibilities included conducting on Sundays and working with the chorus during the week. In the late 1960s, when many shows came to Starlight from somewhere else, Ryan would travel to the "somewhere else," tape the show, and get acquainted with the performers. When he returned to Starlight, the tempo, the style, and the timing of the music were studied so that when the Kansas City musicians gathered for rehearsal, the conductor already knew the proper musical interpretation.

Starlight Theatre was built for operetta. The size of the orchestra pit is sufficiently large to accommodate a big string section. Newer shows coming off Broadway, however, were being written differently than their earlier counterparts. Taking into account the soaring costs of mounting a New York show, composers were penning scores with fewer instruments. *Man of la Mancha,* for example, was written for a small orchestra, while *A Chorus Line*'s score contains no string accompaniment whatsoever. Many post-1950 musicals relied much more heavily on the brass section than on the strings to carry the weight of the melodies. Thus as the decades have passed, the composition of the Starlight orchestra has changed.

The advent of the prepackaged shows in the 1970s disbanded Starlight's large orchestra. The road shows would bring a conductor, a pianist, and percussionist with them, and the remaining instruments (about twenty) were hired from the Kansas City pool of musicians. With only six hours of rehearsal time, the show would go on the boards.

Starlight is a unique place to conduct an orchestra. The voices of the singers on that large stage were sometimes difficult for the conductor to hear. And vice versa. When songs developed right out of the dialogue with no musical introduction, the orchestra's cue notes to the singers onstage were difficult to discern. In the late '60s during one of the after midnight rehearsals, one of the drummers in the orchestra was tired, very tired, and probably thinking about hot coffee and a roll instead of the play being rehearsed onstage. When the moment came for a note to be given so that the singer onstage could find the correct pitch, the drummer sounded the kettledrums. Drums, of course, have no pitch, so the singer was left to his own ingenuity to determine his beginning note. Berger later remarked, "I've been in show business for 666 years and that's the first time I've ever heard a pitch note given by a timpani."

Pesky little insects could make a Starlight evening performance worrisome. During a performance of 1963's *Wild Cat*, a bug flew around Martha Raye's head as she stood on one of the side islands. The lights shining on her made the creature appear even larger. Raye, ever the comedian, pointed up at the insect and quipped, "You should have paid for a ticket." Throughout the years, many of the musicians in the pit echoed that sentiment nightly.

HARDING DORN

During the first nine years of Starlight's history, four different choreographers had been on Dick Berger's production staff. Harding Dorn, who began his Starlight career in 1956 as ensemble director and two years later assumed the responsibilities of choreographer, stayed with Starlight for fifteen years. The style, the vibrancy, the showmanship of Starlight's dances were his invention.

Dorn, a native of New York, began his career at age eleven and a year later danced professionally for the Juilliard School of Music's production of *Joseph and His Brethren*. After high school he performed in the chorus at the Roxy Theatre in New York, appeared in the Chicago company of *Oklahoma!*, and then danced in the Ballet Russe de Monte Carlo for seven years. After a train wreck ended his own performance career, he began choreographing for a variety of theatres around the U.S. as well as Canada, Mexico, and Puerto Rico.

Following summers at Starlight, during the off-season months, Dorn would conduct classes in his Studio of Dance Arts in Woodmere, New York, and in later years instructed students during the winter months in Kansas City. He auditioned young dancers in New York, in Chicago, at Butler University in Indianapolis, and in Kansas City, frequently choosing local dancers for the Starlight experience.

The souvenir program of 1966 described Harding Dorn "as hard driving as he is gifted... [having] the stamina of a professional football player and the patience of a saint as he pulls his individual charges into a polished unit for each of the Starlight productions." His dancers would agree to every adjective but one—patient. Dorn was a hard taskmaster. He was quick, he was brutal, but he was reliable.

Dorn had to be quick and very organized in order to present a different set of dances each week. He

Harding Dorn with ensemble members.

did his homework. Living in New York during the winter months provided the opportunity to see all the shows performed by the best. After the upcoming season's shows had been selected, Dorn would familiarize himself with the script and the music. He would watch old movies and tapes to acquaint himself with the style and flavor of the dance numbers. When he headed for the summer season in Kansas City, he occasionally had written notes for specific dances, especially the "classics" like the "Steam Heat" number from *The Pajama Game.*

PHOTOS COURTESY OF STARLIGHT THEATRE

Left: **Can Can,** 1969.

Above: **Dorothy Coulter** starring in *The Desert Song,* 1966.

Once rehearsals began, Dorn oftentimes would choreograph spontaneously. He had an idea of what he wanted, but he would improvise on the spot, moving his dancers about the stage to get the desired effect.

He was a choreographer who knew all kinds of dance idioms, and, most importantly, how to adapt them to the size of the Starlight stage. Because he was forced to have dancers effectively project his concepts on a stage that was seventy feet wide at the proscenium, movement had to be big, bold, precise, yet distinctive. Many times his dances, which were staged with the idea of wide expansive movements, had to sacrifice intricacy for spectacle. Some of Dorn's dances were too broadly based for his dancers to appreciate.

He was also extremely inventive. Phil de Rosier once remarked that "Harding had talent in his fingernails"—he could choreograph a brisk march, a melting waltz, a sizzling jazz piece, a dynamic can-can, or a comic routine on a pogo stick. He devised movements for dancers on their toes, on roller skates, and even on ostriches. Some of his dances were brilliant. "Belly up to the Bar," a dance Dorn choreographed for *The Unsinkable Molly Brown* in 1963, showcased a remarkable piece of creative imagination. So, too, did the "Rich Kids' Rag" number from the next season's *Little Me.*

But not every number was a show-stopper. In fact, some were stopped before they even got to the show, as was the case with a ballet number in *Bye Bye Birdie* (1962). Chita Rivera was cast as Rosie, the lead female character, and this ballet was to depict Rosie scheming about the ways she "could get rid of" Albert, her unreliable boyfriend. Dorn had scaffolds and a guillotine built, seven coffins mounted on rollers, and included a cannon and multiple rifles for the dancers to carry—in short, a whole raft of expensive props to add to the "drama" of the dance number. The problem was insufficient time to train the dancers to synchronize the movement of all those props. At dress rehearsal, as dancers collided with each other and props were wheeled out at the wrong time, Berger, who was seated in the audience area watching this catastrophe, cried out, "Cut the ballet!" At the production meeting following the rehearsal, Berger

ranted, "Harding, all those props must have cost a fortune. Next time you concoct a number like that, remember this time when I said 'cut it' and don't do it." It was a rare moment, though, for Dorn to make such a misjudgment. Usually he was quite dependable, which is probably why he remained in Dick Berger's good graces.

In the first two weeks of the season, when the dancers' bodies and minds were fresh, Dorn would teach them all the dances for the upcoming show as well as some of the big production numbers scheduled further into the season. He was always working ahead—a necessity for a choreographer who had to devise so many dances for so many shows in so short a time.

In general, Dorn enjoyed good rapport with his dancers. According to Elaine Loughead, his assistant, he "was temperamental, had a good sense of humor, and could pitch a good fit! But he stood up for his dancers. Only *he* could yell at them. Dorn had a big ego like everyone else out there. But the arguments were generally brief, hot, and short-lived. Then it was business as usual." Sometimes during particularly difficult rehearsals, he would crack a joke to ease the tension of the long hours, and sometimes the joke was on him. It was not unknown for him to become so frustrated that he would cram the wrong end of a lighted cigarette into his mouth.

Harding Dorn was devoted to his work. To constantly create required a tireless worker, and he exemplified that. In his later years at Starlight, he also took over some directing responsibilities, including the productions of *My Fair Lady* (1967), *Sweet Charity* (1968), and the 1971 season's *The Unsinkable Molly Brown* and *Funny Girl*. He also did some directing work around town, including productions at the Jewish Community Center.

Top: **Karen Morrow** and the New Christy Minstrels star in *The Unsinkable Molly Brown*, 1963.

Above: **Donald O'Connor** in *Little Me*, 1964.

Right: **Chita Rivera** stars in *Bye Bye Birdie*, 1962.

"Starlight has been my teacher, my university, my doctorate," Dorn remarked in 1971. He returned for so many years to continue his education because he found his love for the theatre satisfied by the all-consuming schedule and challenge of a typical Starlight season.

THE STORY OF STARLIGHT THEATRE

JERRY FUNK

A high school production of *Bringing Up Father* in Coffeyville, Kansas, hooked him. The principal had been drafted for the directing job and he picked Jerry Funk to play the lead. That brush with theatre set the direction of Funk's professional life. His stage managing career at Starlight spanned four decades, encompassing the summer seasons of 1959, 1965-68, 1971-72, and 1979-80. Working under both Dick Berger and Tony Ferrara, Funk amassed a wealth of theatre experience from which to draw.

In a bad week it was possible for him to work a hundred hours. Actors' hours were guarded by the union, but the stage manager had no restrictions on his time. From 9:30 A.M. until whenever, his duties included integrating every technical aspect of a show along with overseeing the performers' cues for entrances and exits during a performance.

Two platforms stood behind the giant act curtain, one on each side of the opening. Funk nightly sat inside the stage right curtain, his eyes glued to a script with every cue noted. During a performance, he rode the curtain and called all the cues for the actors, singers, and dancers, the lights, the sound, and the scene changes. He did not push the button that operated the giant curtain, but he did everything else. He was connected via intercoms to the sound personnel, to the stagehands backstage, to the spotlight operators on the light bridge, to the orchestra area, and to all the backstage dressing rooms.

Starlight's size made the stage manager's job unusual. All of a play's cues in a Broadway house or in the smallest community theatre are called by the stage manager. But because Starlight is so big, and so many scenes played in front of the act curtain where the stage manager could not see them, the lighting coordinator, who sat on the light bridge, would call most of the light cues.

Before a production began, Funk checked all the technical aspects. Were all the lights functioning? Did Mrs. Penelope have her costume on stage right? Was the mike working on the farm set? Had the rifles for the fight scene been found yet? Had the rain from the day's shower been cleaned off the stage? These were only a few of the hundred questions to ask and answer before the curtain parted for Act I. This, however, was his night job. During the day it was his responsibility to work with the carpenters, the electricians, the sound men, the actors, the musicians, the prop people, and the singing and dancing ensemble to ensure that all aspects of the show were coordinated and on schedule.

On Monday, he clocked in by 9:30 A.M. New principals reported for next week's show. Costume fittings as well as promotions and publicity chores were attended to while the principals for the current show had a run-through. After the opening night's performance, a production staff meeting would take place. Perhaps Funk could leave by midnight. Tuesday the new principals would rehearse from ten until five.

Jerald D. Funk, stage manager.

The performance that night of the current show would be over by eleven. Perhaps he would be home by half past. The rest of the week went similarly until Saturday, when a full run-through for the next week's show would take place at midnight. By five o'clock Sunday morning, the cast would have gone, but the technical staff stayed to iron out the problems. Tomorrow was Monday, and new principals for a new show would report. Funk remarked years later that "Starlight was a unique place to work. All that pulling together for a brand new show every week. Everything was so big, big, big, big. The scenic logistics were tremendous—sometimes overwhelming."

Jerry Funk and Harding Dorn inspecting props for the upcoming show of *Kismet*, 1967.

His Starlight season began three weeks before the first performance. Only the staff members reported to the theatre then. During that week they planned, organized, scheduled, and duplicated scores of packets of written material. The next week the chorus arrived for work. The last week before the first performance, the entire cast would assemble for rehearsal. From the first day of reporting until the final curtain call of the season, there was no day off from the responsibilities.

Sometimes Funk had to go beyond the job description. After a performance of *Brigadoon*, one of the principals came storming into Roland Fiore's room in the tunnel and threatened to kill the conductor, who had a penchant for speeding up the tempo without warning or concern for the singers and dancers performing to the rhythm of his baton. That particular evening Fiore lived thanks to the physical presence of Funk, who stood between the principal and the maestro and avoided bloodshed!

Why would anyone choose to have such a summer job? Love of theatre! "There was pride and satisfaction in participating, but there was nothing easy about it," Funk stated ten years after he retired from Starlight. He had plenty of experience. He had acted (over seventy-five roles by the time he graduated from college), taught at the college level, directed summer stock, and worked at Starlight Musicals in Indianapolis and at the New York Shakespearean Festival with Joseph Papp. He had stage managed for Broadway shows, off-Broadway theatres, New York's Phoenix Theatre and American Plays Theatre, touring companies, and the Kansas City Lyric Opera. That vast array of skills was brought to bear on the biggest project of them all—running the Swope Park theatre for a summer season.

As Funk wanted to stay in Kansas City year-round, he decided to open his own business. He chose a business partner whose Starlight career lasted nearly two decades and who holds the Starlight record for most performances by a supporting actress, Lilian Armijo. Together he and his wife Lilian opened Backstage Workshop, an actor and singer training school located on Ward Parkway Plaza Street. They remain devoted to the theatre and to the people who create for it, and especially to the people who made Starlight such a special place to be.

ROBERT BENSTEAD

Phil de Rosier's ideas were greatly enhanced by the ability of another fine artist who worked in the paint shop. Robert Benstead was able to take a scene from de Rosier's twelve-by-eighteen-inch rendering and transfer it to an eighty-foot wide set of stretched muslin flats. Translating that small drawing onto giant-sized scenery was an artistic skill unto itself, and nobody did it better than Benstead. "He was the best scenic artist I've ever seen," remarked Randy Halsey, Starlight's present master carpenter, "and he had a wealth of knowledge and ability and was able to put it into practice."

Benstead, a native of Missouri, began his Starlight career as a dancer in the 1950 "Thrills of the Century" pageant. In 1954 he began work in the scene shop. During the winter months, Benstead was employed in New York by the Mayflower Scenic Studio. He could easily have done well in the Broadway theatres, but he was content to come to Kansas City each summer and work. He stayed with Starlight for thirty years until his death in 1980. An expert in Indian lore and dancing, he also was active in the Boy Scouts for three decades. This fine talent was personally responsible for transforming de Rosier's artistic imagination onto scenery for the enjoyment of nearly eight thousand persons per performance.

Robert Benstead, scenic artist.

ANCEL LACY, HERB OBERMEYER, RANDY HALSEY

Ancel Lacy "was a top drawer craftsman—a top drawer human being," reported Phil de Rosier nearly forty years after first meeting Lacy. He also was a quiet man. He didn't partake of alcohol, didn't smoke, didn't drink coffee. He didn't even own a suit. He had to buy one for Al Krikorian's wedding.

Lacy was born in Carthage, Missouri, and lived in a house that backed up to the stage door of the Grand Opera House, home to numerous touring stock companies and road shows. His mother died when he was very young and he was practically reared by the stagehands. He considered himself a stagehand by the age of twelve. In 1922, when the stagehands' local was formed in Carthage, Lacy became a charter member. Two years later he began working in Kansas City at the old Shubert Theatre, the Convention Hall, and the Ararat Temple. Traveling on then to Detroit, he had the good fortune to study there under Hiram Cornell. He returned to Carthage to become a movie theatre owner, but when the temporary opening of the Main Street Theatre occurred in 1939, Lacy returned to Kansas City, never to leave the live theatrical scene again.

PHOTOS COURTESY OF STARLIGHT THEATRE

Ancel Lacy, master carpenter.

The Artists and Technicians

75

Carpenters at work. *Left to right:* John Hogan, Ed Maier, and Herman Obermeyer.

PHOTO COURTESY OF BURT OBERMEYER

In 1951, when Dick Berger was searching for a master carpenter who could take on the responsibility of building his young theatre's huge sets and the wagons on which to mount them, local workmen pointed to Lacy as the best man in the business. Berger was never disappointed. He later commented that Lacy was "the finest stage carpenter I've ever seen. We don't have to worry about bringing stage carpenters from New York because there aren't any there who are equal to Lacy."

In addition to his regular responsibilities, Lacy designed and built the act curtain that was used for over thirty years. After the curtain was installed, no one could figure out how to wire it properly. For the first several weeks, it had to be opened and closed manually. The electrical company in charge of wiring it could not resolve the problems. Finally, when they had retreated from the scene in frustration, Lacy went to work and wired the curtain himself.

The outstanding sets in those first years were due partly to Lacy's abilities to plan and implement. Albert Johnson, the 1951 designer for Starlight, gave Lacy very detailed plans for each set. The process, while very thorough, was very time-consuming for the designer. The following year, when Phil de Rosier came to the theatre, he would give Lacy a much more abbreviated version of the set plans, and Lacy would convert those plans into reality.

He also took charge of an overnight addition to the front of the stage in 1958 when Jerry Lewis insisted that he wasn't close enough to the audience. Lacy telephoned salesman Ross of the Tamm Lumber Company at two o'clock in the morning and ordered enough lumber for the addition. He wanted it by eight o'clock the next morning! (The boards arrived at the theatre on time.) Lacy and his crew of ten carpenters labored under the blazing sun in 100-degree heat to assemble a stage fifty feet wide and measuring twenty-four feet from the footlights to the first audience row. The stage was ready for performance that night.

When Ancel Lacy retired, his protégé took the position. Herman Obermeyer was fifty years old when he came to Starlight with the intention of working for just a few days. He stayed for twenty-four years. When Starlight first opened, Obermeyer was a teacher in a trade school instructing post-World War II students. He knew welding, and in 1951 Starlight needed someone who could build the rails for the huge act curtain. He was contacted and offered the job. He enjoyed working at the theatre so much that he never left. In 1974 when a heart attack left him unable to work, he lay in bed and, according to his son Burt, shed tears of regret that his summers at Starlight were over.

Obermeyer managed people well and frequently took the newcomers "under his wing." He and his crew would be the first to arrive at Starlight in the spring. They would build and repair the scenery dollies, repair any broken spots in the orchestra pit, and construct all the frames for the flats needed in the upcoming season. In the 1950s and '60s, a crew of fifteen men was needed for the backstage carpentry; during the '70s, only ten men were employed.

In 1975 Randy Halsey became the youngest master carpenter in Starlight's history. At the time, he was a twenty-eight-year-old graduate of the University of Missouri at Kansas City in neuropsychology. He had worked his way through college at Starlight during the summers. Halsey's first acquaintance with the theatre came as a patron who would often bring a date to see the productions. He dearly loved the theatre experience long before he ever knew he would become a part of it. Even today he approaches his job with the eyes and heart of a patron.

Ancel Lacy and Herman Obermeyer were "old school, country boy, shade-tree mechanics who knew how to work with their hands," Halsey declared. But the time of unlimited inexpensive labor has long since passed. The approach today has to be different. Preplanning must take place in order to minimize the man hours needed to complete a task. Halsey's future plans include working at the theatre "as long as they'll have me, as long as I can contribute all I can and make them three to four times what they pay me." With that kind of an attitude, Starlight will continue to present top quality sets—that same excellence initiated by Ancel Lacy, continued by Herb Obermeyer, and ever-present today because of Randy Halsey's efforts.

Randy Halsey, present master carpenter.

AL KRIKORIAN

From 1957 until 1988, Al Krikorian walked through the back gates of Starlight every summer season. He began his career there as a stagehand, but within a few years he found his true calling. Krikorian was a marvelous scavenger. He knew where every unusual item within the Kansas City area might be found and who might loan it to Starlight for a week or two. It was a knack with a perfect outlet: Krikorian became a superlative prop master.

The properties man was responsible for finding a wide assortment of items needed for the set or for the actors' use, taking care of those items, making certain they were in the right place at the right time during the performance, and returning them to their proper owners. He did all those jobs well.

He was first recommended for the job by Charles Lamonica, the prop man before him. When Krikorian accepted the position, he did so with the idea that he would never be outwitted by a set designer who demanded too much. He would find every requested piece, no matter how farfetched or how spectacular. He accepted the friendly challenge and never left Phil de Rosier wanting. Find a real presidential flag for *Mr. President*, 1964. (He found one in Harry Truman's Presidential Library.) Find a genuine brass cash register for *The Unsinkable Molly Brown*. See if you can locate a century-old whatnot shelf for *The Music Man*, and while you're at it, how about seventy-six trombones for the town band! Krikorian did all that and much more.

Familiar with antique dealers and curators of the local museums and art galleries, he also would borrow period furniture items from prominent Mission Hills homes. He even lent his own furniture to Ethel Merman to use in the dressing rooms on either side of the stage specifically designed for her use in *Call Me Madam* (1968). For *State Fair* (1969), he "pirated" a 1927 wagon from a local dairy. When the paint shop began to apply another color to it, he had to rescue the borrowed treasure. For the 1970 production of *Fiddler on the Roof*, all the items for worship were genuine, having been secured from a local synagogue for Starlight's use. The camouflage equipment for *South Pacific* in 1968 had to be shipped from the Army bases in Wichita, Kansas. Finding crystal chandeliers, authentic Old West rifles, .22 caliber rifle blanks, and twenty-six banjos was all in a day's work. The elephant and ostrich needed for *Around the World in Eighty Days* also showed up on his "Please Find" list.

On the Wednesday two weeks before a show opened, Krikorian would receive his prop list from de Rosier. All the props had to be in the theatre by Friday so that the actors had use of them during the next week's rehearsals. He would spend hours on the telephone locating the exact items needed; that done, he would have to go pick up the items, load them into a truck, and bring them to the theatre. When a show was over, he would reverse the process, reloading the items to return them to their proper

Prop crew. *Left to right:* Joe Antonello, Rick Berger, Bill Brown, Al Krikorian, Charles Lamonica and set designer Phil de Rosier.

owners. He would also begin again to canvass the town for another group of "rare gems" needed for the upcoming production.

Ability to get along with people was a must for a man who wanted to take one's favorite piece of furniture or priceless antique and not give a dime in return. No props were ever purchased while Krikorian was on the job. People were talked out of their prized possessions by a promise of free tickets and his word that the items would be returned intact.

When he had obtained all the necessary props for a show, the other half of his job entailed running them during the performance. That part of the job, in later years, he left to his son Mike. The night prop crew would come in ninety minutes before show time and start to arrange props on the various sets. As the show ran along, the crew kept putting away props and arranging upcoming sets. A day's work was finished when the act curtain closed for the final time and the last prop was safely stored away for the next performance.

When the proper item could not be found because no such thing existed (as in the case of a pumpkin carriage for Cinderella), the artificer made those items in the Starlight workshop. James Craig, Bill Brown, Tim Hartnett, Chuck Chaffee, and Pat Morris have held that position throughout the years.

Craig was a Kansas City stagehand long before Starlight Theatre ever was built. In the early 1920s he constructed the Priest of Pallas floats for the Merchant Association's parade, as well as built shows in all the small towns around the area. He would enter the big display tent in the town square or sometimes in an open field and chalk off the different areas used by the various businessmen for display. Craig, ever interested in catching the roving eye, also would make certain to build a posing platform for the girls to stand on and strike a beautiful pose. Craig finished out his life by making interesting props for Starlight audiences. He was still employed at the theatre when he celebrated his eighty-fifth birthday.

James Craig, artificer. Craig was the oldest employee of Starlight Theatre (85 years old).

His position was taken over by Bill Brown, whose father, Walter Brown, was the first master production carpenter. Brown continued the fine tradition of masterful props, fashioning lampposts, draperies, ornamental chairs, gondolas, mango trees, stagecoaches, and hundreds of other items before he relinquished his post to Tim Hartnett in 1969. Hartnett turned the job over to Chuck Chaffee until 1981, when Pat Morris assumed the responsibilities. Throughout all those years, while the Starlight workshop was engaged in building distinctive properties, Krikorian was busy snooping through the city's nooks and crannies in order to locate the perfect prop for Starlight's next show.

Krikorian stayed at Starlight Theatre for more than three decades because he thoroughly enjoyed what he was doing. After his retirement, he confessed, "My contribution to Starlight was one of the biggest accomplishments of my life." Who could say that any better?

COSTUMES

MISS AUDRE AND VIRGINIA DONOVAN

During the 1950s and '60s, the elegant costumes seen on the Starlight stage were not made at the theatre, but rather were designed and stitched in New York and shipped from there. They were all the creation of a single woman—Audre Nethercott, but only the postman bothered with her last name. She was known in the theatrical circles as Miss Audre.

Miss Audre worked for the Eaves Costume Company, which celebrated its hundredth anniversary in 1963. The company was founded by Albert G. Eaves, who had served a theatrical apprenticeship as prop and makeup man with the pioneer Edison movie studio in New Jersey, historically known as the Black Maria. Eaves began his business in the old theatre center in Manhattan, Union Square. In time his business moved uptown to the theatre district near Forty-second Street. One of his employees, Charles Geoly, bought the firm from him, and Geoly's sons were running the business when Richard Berger first contacted them about costuming for Starlight Theatre.

PHOTO COURTESY OF STARLIGHT THEATRE
Julius LaRosa struggles with Kate as Joe Macaulay looks on. *Kiss Me Kate*, 1958.

Miss Audre designed thousands of costumes for the Swope Park theatre, but she saw only two performances on the great stage. Her last visit occurred when Berger invited her to view the production of *Hello, Dolly!* in 1970. Her usual modus operandi was to get the script from Berger in New York, read through the play, study the characters and their actions, have a discussion with him on costume ideas, and then make color renderings of each costume. Next she would make up a muslin pattern, indicating how each character would look. After receiving

THE STORY OF STARLIGHT THEATRE

Left: **The ensemble** suitably attired for *My Fair Lady*, 1964.

Below: **The Music Man's** River City youngster in need of Virginia Donovan's services.

a nod from the producer, she would proceed to have the costumes made in the workrooms of the New York firm. Occasionally, some of the principal characters would come into the shop for fittings.

Her designs always had to be suited to the Starlight budget. She often would substitute less expensive materials for ones that were too costly. For example, sequined gowns sometimes were replaced with lamé, which reflected the light but could be highlighted with spray rhinestones. Designing for Starlight differed from designing for New York theatres because of the size. Miss Audre used more vibrant colors and wider styled lines for her Starlight designs because part of the audience sat so far from the actors. After Miss Audre's creations were assembled, they were shipped by train to Kansas City in large trunks. The ten to fifteen trunks of costumes were picked up by the Israel Trucking Firm each Monday morning and delivered to the theatre. There they had to be unpacked, hung, and sorted by Virginia Donovan, the first lady of wardrobe for Starlight Theatre.

Donovan was born in southern Missouri. After traveling to Chicago to try her luck with a modeling career, she returned to Kansas City. Here she met and married Cyril "Duggie" Donovan, a Kansas City stagehand who served as president of Local #31 for twenty-two years and as its business agent for three more until his death in 1956. She began working backstage in costumes for numerous road shows that came through Kansas City. In 1951 she was asked to take charge of wardrobe at Starlight Theatre.

Her day began at ten in the morning and ended when the evening's final applause was only a memory. On Mondays she would fit the principals of the next week's show. Sometimes entire wardrobes had to be redone. Later in the week the chorus members would stop by the costume shop in order to be fitted. All costumes had to be

The Artists and Technicians

Virginia Donovan, wardrobe mistress.

pressed and assembled in the proper dressing rooms, though that was only part of her job. Donovan had to stay every night of performance to help dress characters or be available for last minute alterations. Not infrequently Berger would witness the dress rehearsal on Saturday at midnight, see some inadequate costume on stage, and cry out, "Phil, do something with that—costume." The next day, Sunday afternoon, Phil de Rosier and Virginia Donovan would take over the costume shop, redesigning some character's wardrobe.

On sweltering hot days the costume shop, located in the small metal building next to the cafeteria, became an oven. Temperatures could sometimes reach 120 degrees, but Donovan never complained. Finally an air conditioner was donated to the shop, and Donovan's son, Harold Childers, the master electrician at Starlight for fifteen years, ran wiring from the pylon area in order to operate it.

Donovan enjoyed her work. The association with talented people and the feeling of belonging were the driving forces behind her choice of a career. "I wouldn't want to do anything else for a living," she confided in 1960. "When you're with the members of a cast for a while, you begin to love them." Although she was also the wardrobe mistress for the Chicago Ballet Company and for the American Royal Coronation Ball in Kansas City, Starlight was her first love. Over thirty-five thousand costumes passed through her hands before her position was assumed by Ann Sheets in 1964.

During the 1970s, most of the traveling companies brought their own costumes with them. The costumes usually arrived at Starlight the day prior to the dress rehearsal. The wardrobe mistress and her assistants would unpack and press each costume—a time-consuming task considering that roughly two hundred costumes were used each week.

In the 1980s, costumes were rented from the Eaves-Brooks company in New York. No personal attention was given to the making or the designing of the garb. After a show was chosen and the principal characters cast, members of the performing company were measured for costumes. A measurement sheet containing all pertinent information was sent to the New York firm, and costumes in trucks were promptly forthcoming.

RAY MAIER

What would Starlight Theatre be without adequate acoustics? How popular could the theatre be if the audience could not hear the performers? These questions claimed paramount importance for the early planners.

When Starlight first was built, the North Kansas City Electric Company sent Art Wearth to install all the RCA equipment. RCA engineers checked out the system and determined that the sound was as good as could be expected using war surplus cables and intercoms. Ray Maier, however, the sound technician at the theatre from 1954 to 1980, made a lot of improvements over the years.

Maier is part of a family theatre tradition that began with his father Ed. Ed Maier began working the scary "Blood and Thunder" shows at the old Gillis Theater at age thirteen and continued stagehand work all of his life. He worked as a flyman at the Shubert, a light man at the Midland, and then came to Starlight in 1951 to contribute his talents. He was the second oldest employee of Starlight Theatre when he died at the age of eighty-one.

His son Ray was a born electrical wizard. While in grade school Ray Maier made his first crystal set. At Kansas City's Northeast High School, he built amplifiers and rented them out for spare cash. He attended Finlay Engineering College and studied electronics, which, in turn he used during his stint with the Army Signal Corps in the Pacific. When he returned to his hometown after the war, he was employed by several companies before securing permanent status with WDAF-TV; but he also wanted to use his electrical wizardry in the world of theatre. Maier ran the spotlights for the Ice Capades, for performances at the Orpheum Theatre, and for the Lyric Opera. He started his Starlight career in 1951 as an extra stagehand building scenery; in 1954 he became the assistant sound technician, and in 1958, the man in charge.

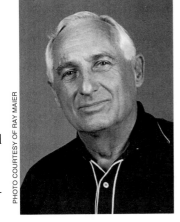

Ray Maier, soundman.

PHOTO COURTESY OF RAY MAIER

Positioning sound equipment for an outdoor theatre is no easy matter. "Little things" could cause havoc. If it rained, or looked like rain, all the microphones had to be covered with plastic. If the wind was blowing, a constant noise might arise in all the mikes. If a performer stood at a certain spot in between the footlight microphones, the mikes would cancel each other out and a "dead spot" would occur—no one could hear the performer's efforts, even though he or she stood within a few feet of sound equipment. During the winter months, when it was idle, the equipment had to be stored in a room with electric heaters and dehumidifiers running constantly. In the summertime the heat created by the presence of so many bodies in the audience area sometimes caused a layer of cooler air to settle a few feet above the patrons' heads, and the sound waves projecting from the stage would take the course of least resistance and sail up and away from the paying public's ears.

Throughout Maier's tenure, new systems, new equipment, and new positions were tried in order to provide the best possible sound. The sound system got an overhaul in

The Artists and Technicians   83

1965 and again in 1973. During the early 1950s, nine microphones placed in the footlights were up in the air several feet and could be seen easily by the audience. Eventually "shotgun" microphones were placed in the footlight trough so as to catch the sound of the performers but not the sight of the audience.

Wireless mikes made their debut at Starlight in 1963 when Connie Stevens starred in *The Wizard of Oz*. Although she had a wonderful singing voice, the producer was worried that she would not project sufficiently to allow the entire audience to hear. Maier sent to Greenwich, Connecticut, to rent the third prototype wireless mike ever made. The wireless Comrex was sent to Starlight within the day, and Miss Stevens had her sound booster on for the first performance. Starlight purchased that mike, followed in later years by Swintek wireless microphones. By 1980 the principal characters in a show used seven wireless microphones.

Maier disliked the wireless wonders because they were so unpredictable. The cords could come loose, and at times the mikes could give static. When a performer would perspire on those hot summer nights, the salt would affect the sound. And when love scenes heated up, cannon-like sounds as well as "fireworks" could go off when the couple embraced. As a sound man, Maier remarked that "you could never take your eyes off the stage. You had to concentrate every minute."

Maier and his assistant were located in the sound room at the west base of the light bridge tower in the back of the audience area. They were connected by intercom to the stage manager, who rode the act curtain each night, to the assistant stage manager on stage left, to the lighting technicians' room at the base of the west pylon, to the lighting director located on the light bridge, and to the orchestra leader. Prompt and accurate communication among all those people was necessary to running the show smoothly. If the intercom system was faulty, so were light and sound cues throughout the performance. For this reason the intercom system always remained of first concern to Maier and his crew.

Maier was responsible for the sound from the microphones on stage and on the principal characters. There were nine mikes in the footlight trough, one or two mikes on either island off each side of the stage, and tunnel mikes that projected sound cues from both right and left tunnels. In addition, generally three but sometimes as many as five mikes hung on the huge sets, and, for the smaller interior scenes, several microphones were suspended from the scene wagons. All those devices Maier controlled from the sound room. As a performer moved, the mikes behind him or her were turned down and those ahead were turned up. At the end of a scene, Maier would "kill" the stage mikes as soon as the lights went off. When the great traveling curtain was closed, the two or three men on the stage sound crew would disconnect the mikes from the previous scene, wait for the new scenery to

This scene from *Up in Central Park*, 1953, shows the old elevated mikes.

PHOTO COURTESY OF JOHN DOOHAN

THE STORY OF STARLIGHT THEATRE

Left: **Shotgun mikes** in evidence during a rehearsal of *How to Succeed in Business Without Really Trying,* 1966.

Below: **The light canopy** built over Starlight's stage in 1983.

be rolled on stage, then connect the new mikes needed for the upcoming scene. The crew had to take care that the casters on the huge scene wagons did not roll over the stage cables and crush them. Although there were usually from twenty-five to thirty-five mikes used for a production, only two or three mikes were live at any given time. If all this sounds complicated, it's because it was.

Maier's assistant, positioned in the sound room, took charge of "riding" the orchestra. The crew balanced all the orchestra mikes for opening night and then generally did not tinker with them during the run of the show. Each section of the orchestra had its own microphone. The strings, the woodwinds, the brass, the drums, and the piano were all sub mastered and run together for the master control in the sound room. Maier's assistant would kill the sound of the orchestra after each number so that the audience could not hear the coughing noises and comments of the orchestra members. When the maestro raised his baton, the controls were brought up so that the swell of music could fill the air.

When the theatre changed producers in 1981, all the former equipment was torn out. Bass horns in the towers were taken away. The stage cables were cut with bolt cutters. Management hired a company from Tennessee that specialized in rock

Vivien Ferrara with boys in a scene from *Peter Pan*, 1969.

concerts to redo the sound system. Unfortunately for the patrons, the equipment that works well for a rock show proves inadequate for the distance miking required in a play or musical. In 1983 a canopy was built over the stage area, which greatly aided sound problems. For the first time in Starlight's history, microphones could be hung over the center of the stage.

Surprises occurred occasionally, such as in 1969 when Ruta Lee starred in *Peter Pan*. One particular night she was standing offstage wearing a wireless mike, watching Wendy fly into the nursery. The machinery operator who controlled the cables allowed Wendy to glide into the room but left her suspended several feet in the air before plopping her onto the stage (fortunately in an upright position). Miss Lee uttered a few choice expletives about the mental capacity of the stagehand who had dropped the girl, played by Vivien Ferrara. Lee's mike was live and the audience heard every word she said. As she was out of sight in the tunnel, however, the audience assumed those bawdy remarks arose from little Vivien, standing rather startled on stage. What a headache for a sound man!

Headaches, backaches, heartaches, and all, Starlight was the place Maier chose to be for thirty summers of his life. He respected Richard Berger and years later confessed that "he couldn't have asked for a better man to work for than Tony Ferrara." Ten years after he retired from Starlight, Maier reflected, "I often thought how fortunate I was to be sitting there working those shows. I loved it! I loved working with those wonderful people with those great voices who put their hearts and souls into doing their best. I felt like I was part of it."

LIGHTMEN

BURT OBERMEYER AND DAVID MILLER

"I couldn't imagine a summer without Starlight, not at this house anyway," declared Marlene Obermeyer, daughter-in-law of Herb Obermeyer, wife of master electrician Burt Obermeyer, and mother of five sons who have worked at Starlight over the years. For this family, summer and Starlight are synonymous. The history of the family's involvement goes back to the beginning of the theatre, when father Herb arrived as a temporary employee.

Burt Obermeyer began his Starlight career as a stagehand. He didn't want to follow

THE STORY OF STARLIGHT THEATRE

in his father's footsteps as a carpenter or welder, so in 1974 he took the master electrician job at night during the summers. His boss at the Bendix plant was very understanding when he had to leave his regular job to go to an afternoon rehearsal or setup at Starlight—-just another example of how the community supported the workings of the theatre.

In the late 1980s, when the University of Missouri was mounting an exhibit of old theatre equipment, Starlight was contacted and asked to donate its 1960s dimmer board. "No way," cried master electrician Obermeyer. "We're still using it." 'Tis true! Other boards have been added to it, but the old dinosaur still pulls its weight. Obermeyer operates the dimmer board from a room in the bottom of the west pylon. His crew includes an assistant, an auxiliary board operator, two deck electricians who unplug and replug lighting units on the stage, two men on the pylons (one on each side), and four men on the huge lighting bridge at the rear of the theatre.

"Burt Obermeyer is loyal to the bone," stated lighting designer Kirk Bookman. That loyalty was sorely tested one year. When Obermeyer first came to work in 1965, Robert Hennessey was in charge of the stagehands. He told the young hire, "This job is for seven nights a week, ten weeks, no time off, and don't be late!" Obermeyer remembered those exact words, and when he became boss of a crew he told them the same thing. One summer when his son was working for him, the young man needed to take a few days off. Obermeyer fired him on the spot.

When Starlight first opened, Evans Electric put in all the equipment and the theatre bought it. Twenty-five 3000-watt Dynabeams projected light from the bridge, while nine 2000-watt klieg lights equipped with framing shutters shone in each of the pylons. At the proscenium entrance, both sides of the stage held a vertical row of nine 2000-watt spotlights. The footlights were made up of a row of thirty 500-watt Fresnel spotlights. In addition to the permanent lighting, auxiliary equipment threw more illumination on stage. Huge "light trees" or "light towers," which were moveable units backstage, could focus light on the playing area from the sides. Sometimes the production called for situating lights on the backstage buildings, in the scene wagons, or on the floor of stage right and left "shin busters."

Unlike the sound equipment, which is stored indoors when not in use, the lights hang out in the Kansas City summer heat and rain for the entire season. Many would become rusty and water filled by September. Consequently, starting in the 1980s, the theatre began renting the lights for each season. By renting rather than owning, the lighting designer gets just what he wants for each new season, and all the equipment comes back in the spring in excellent working order.

The amount of equipment used now in a typical production is staggering. Because of the great width of the stage and depth of the audience area, hundreds of lights illuminate the players. Since 1983 when the new canopy was constructed, most of the stage lighting is located above the actors' heads. Within that canopy four pipes can

PHOTO COURTESY OF TROY THOMAS PHOTOGRAPHY

Burt Obermeyer, master electrician at Starlight for many years.

hold thirty-six lights each. Lighting instruments also hang inside as well as on racks outside the pylons.

A lot of electricity flows through the thirty-five hundred feet of cable at Starlight. For example, the 1990 production of *Oklahoma!* used 219 lamps. If all the lamps hanging at the theatre in 1990 were turned to full flood, they would provide enough light to illuminate a small city on a cold dark night.

The Starlight crew uses various kinds of lighting instruments: par can and Lekos, which project a heavy beam of light from the overhead canopy; ACLUs (aircraft landing units) in the pylons; Dynabeams from the bridge, which flood the stage with general lighting; and, of course, the follow spots, which have showcased many a familiar performing talent for the Starlight audiences.

Each production requires a different lighting plot. In order to obtain just the right amount of light, focused exactly on the correct area, and to project the precise color onto the stage, lighting crews start hanging and focusing lights when it is dark and they work until "they drop." In the 1950s and '60s, this lighting preparation took place at the Saturday midnight rehearsal. In the 1980s and '90s, the crew usually hangs the lights on the Friday or Saturday night prior to the dress rehearsal. Kirk Bookman, the current lighting designer, reported that "the Muny and Indianapolis have more money and better boards. But their budget does not allow time to focus and plan. Starlight's Bob Rohlf allows for that."

From the dimmer boards, Obermeyer and his assistant control the lights in the canopy and on the pylons as well as the Dynabeams on the bridge. Eighty-two circuits patch into the dimmer boards, but the system is not computerized. Every cue must be programmed into the system manually each night. An average show at Starlight has between 110 to 115 different lighting cues per show. Perfect timing and focused concentration are a must for this job.

Obermeyer does not control the follow spots. Those lighting instruments perform under the control of other professionals who have earned their stripes with the theatre. One of those veterans is David Miller. He, too, began his Starlight association in 1951. Both of his sons, David Michael and John, have followed his lead and operated the huge spotlights. During the early '70s, all three Millers worked the bridge at the same time (Bobby Taylor was the only non-Miller in attendance.) In fact, taking into account their uncle's (Ed Purcell) stint as a stagehand in the early '50s, the Miller family can clock over a hundred years of service to Starlight.

Those first years on the bridge offered times of invention and experimentation for Miller and the other operators. One of the original spotlights, a Metro-Genarko, had been bequeathed by the old Orpheum Theatre. Kansas City workman ingenuity kept it and three other follow spots (carbon arc types) operating for years. The crew fashioned chimneys, for example, to allow the extreme heat to escape. Sights built for the lights allowed the operators to pinpoint a performer's head accurately from three hundred feet away. New parts were made when the old pieces rusted out, and fresh paint was applied when the weathering process took its toll.

Spotlight operators on the light bridge. Left to right: Herb Obermeyer, Dave Miller, Bob Newton, and Frank Thomas.

Perching so high off the ground on the hillside gave Miller the opportunity to forewarn the crew about bad weather. Sometimes when he felt a little breeze on the back of his neck he knew strong winds were coming. He was connected via headphones to the stage manager, whom he would call and alert about the approaching storm. Within minutes the stagehands would have the huge scene wagons tied down to the anchors embedded in the stage. More often than not the winds would soon arrive.

Wind on the bridge always presented a problem. The gusty air would sometimes enter the casings and blow out the fan in the lighting instrument. Then the bulb would go out. When that occurred, the other operators had to focus automatically on the main lead character. The powerful currents of air would sometimes "readjust" the huge Dynabeam lights. Following the script also offered quite a challenge. Holding a copy in hand was out of the question. For several years Miller and the other operators

The Artists and Technicians

EXAMPLES OF COMMUNITY SUPPORT FOR STARLIGHT THEATRE

Right: **Damn Yankees** chorus members getting tips from the Kansas City Royals players.

Below right: **Window** of Jenkins Music Company.

Below: **Starlight** shares its star with baseball fans, 1960.

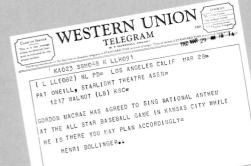

THE STORY OF STARLIGHT THEATRE

used a wooden box with rollers in the top and bottom ends so they could turn the script scroll-fashion. Also not an ideal solution. By the mid-'50s, the lighting director, who was seated up on the bridge, gave the cues to them. One year a heavy canvas wall was constructed in back of the operators to shield them from the north winds. The first strong gusts ripped off the barrier, causing it to fall into the hot lamps and nearly catch fire. So ended the saga of a temporary shield.

When new Xenon instruments were purchased, Miller and company could not operate the lights from the same side of the casing as they had the old spots. They could not "sight down" like they could with the old Genarkos. Miller had to devise other means of detection to find his lighting target. Facial features were indistinguishable on a figure that appeared to be a half inch high. What the player wore thus became the key to finding him or her on the stage. Peering down through the blackness of night at the faint tiny shadows, Miller had to sense the location of his target and then beam the light. If a change in costume or entrance was not passed along to him, dialogue would get swallowed up in the darkness surrounding the performer.

Light attracts bugs! Lots of bugs! Multiple insect bites became an occupational hazard for David Miller and Robert Hennessey, the only two spotlight operators in 1951. For several summers after the '51 flood, the bugs were giant-size and their bites especially painful. Although Hennessey fashioned a sort of beekeeper's bonnet to protect himself, the pests found their way inside his hat anyway. Both men would go home with huge welts on their arms. Netting used over the operators' heads eventually proved somewhat successful.

If Edward Delk forgot anything in his grand design for Starlight, it was an elevator for the light tower. In the early days, all those heavy instruments were hoisted to the bridge by means of hand-over-hand rope pulling by the man at the top. Since that time, a pulley system lifts the lamps up and down. When not in use, the crew stores the spots in rooms on either side of the bridge and in one below the bridge in the west tower.

When Miller first came to the Swope Park theatre, he inscribed "There are always four arcs burning" on the wall of the room west of the bridge. Those words remain there over forty years later, a reminder to all spot personnel that vigilance is mandatory and that lighting consistency spells the hallmark of excellence in the big Starlight Theatre. Obermeyer would heartily agree!

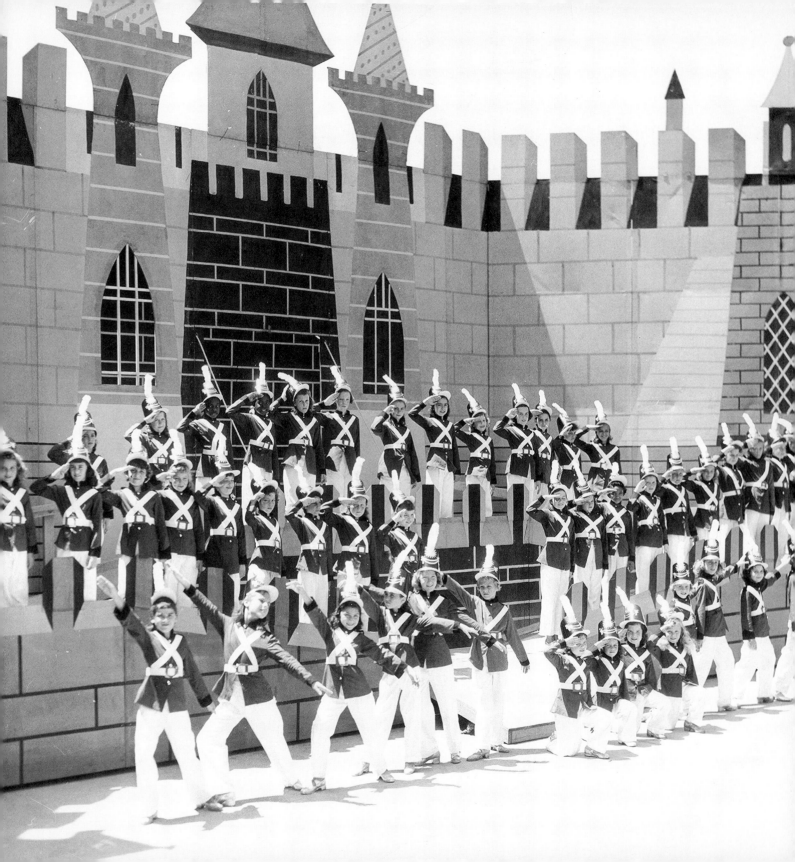

Training Ground for Young Talent

Theatre is not a recess from life. It is the heart of the school of life.
Everett Thorne, brother-in-law of the author.

Starlight Theatre has had a profound effect on the culture of America's Heartland. Performances at the Swope Park theatre have brought the finest American musicals to over eleven million people who have passed through its gates. Not only has Starlight introduced its audience members to great musical pieces, but the theatre offered a highly prized opportunity for young talent to participate in top notch productions and to prepare for the demanding world of professional performance. Many a young artist has graduated from the Starlight stage to succeed in a variety of performing arts endeavors across this country.

Charles Nelson Reilly got his professional start as an ensemble member at Starlight. Later he portrayed the wacky dentist in the 1959 production of *The Bells Are Ringing*. **Meredith** and **Heather MacRae**, daughters of Gordon and Sheila MacRae, made their stage debut in *Annie Get Your Gun* (1960).

William Ledbetter from Parsons, Kansas, who was a member of the Starlight singing ensemble from 1958-61, went on to perform with the Metropolitan Opera in New York, as did **Sandra Warfield**. She performed the lead role in the 1955 production of *Naughty Marietta*.

Dean Dittmann, a Midwest actor born in Frontenac, Kansas, appeared in productions of *The Music Man* (1962), *The Wizard of Oz* (1963), *My Fair Lady* (1964) and *How to Succeed in Business Without Really Trying* (1966). He went on to perform on Broadway, in movies, and in the television series "Highway to Heaven," "Cheers," and "Designing Women."

Charles Rule, a New Yorker who was in the Starlight ensemble in 1959 and 1960, appeared in many Broadway productions including the original casts of *Fiddler on the Roof* and *Phantom of the Opera* in which he is still performing. **Ron Highley**, who

Left: **The chorus** of *Babes in Toyland*, 1951, the first children's show at Starlight Theatre. Chorus names on page 94.

ZORBA •SEVEN BRIDES FOR SEVEN BROTHERS • A FUNNY THING HAPPENED ON THE WAY TO THE FORUM •SUGAR • I DO! I DO! • BALLROOM • THE WIZ •BUBBLING BROWN SUGAR • ANYTHING GOES • 4 GIRLS 4 • GREASE • THE BEST LITTLE WHOREHOUSE IN TEXAS • AIN'T MISBEHAVIN' • ANNIE • THEY'RE PLAYING OUR SONG • JESUS CHRIST SUPERSTAR • A CHORUS LINE • EVITA • HAIR • DANCIN' • GYPSY • MY ONE AND ONLY • 42ND STREET • BIG RIVER AND THE ADVENTURES OF HUCKLEBERRY FINN •

Right, clockwise: **Charles Nelson Reilly,** Meredith MacRae, and Walter Hook.
Below right: **Ron Highley** and Nancy Dussault in *On a Clear Day You Can See Forever.*

The chorus of *Babes in Toyland* included: Judy Allsup, Bill Anthony, Judy Anthony, Gwendolyn Barker, Donna Barton, Billie Ann Burnadell, Linda Lee Bleich, Patty Bova, Judy Boyce, Mary Jane Boyles, Lynn Bush, Judy Curd, Joan Cusak, Patricia Damanti, Kathe Decker, Linda Depasco, Teresa Ann Depasco, Juliana Doohan, Monica Doohan, Carol Douglas, Linda Douglas, Barbara Edwards, Diane Flynn, Penny Golden, Jacque Grace, Adrienne Gray, Andrea Gray, Kathy Hall, Patricia Hanlon, Spunky Hanney, Peggy Harris, Kathleen Hegarty, Mary Frances Hiller, Charlene Jones, Martha Kelley, Patty Koch, Peggy Krouse, Martha Law, Rochelle Lerner, Tina Lerner, Gae Lindsay, Barbara Loman, Patty Martin, Barbara Ann Matherly, Francis Ann Meader, Vicki Rae Molleson, Anne Moore, Elaine Moore, Ronald Olson, Ann O'Neill, Suzanne Pruitt, Clara Jo Reed, Shirley Reisbord, Sally Jo Rings, David Rizer, Rebecca Roop, Jean Satchell, Bonnie Shilling, Sally Schirmer, Vicki Sue Schlichter, Judith Schwartz, Patty Shafer, Ruby Lee Snider, Vicki Ann Staab, Ann Stutzman, Myron Stutzman, Pamela Kay Tandy, Barbara Vanneman, Carol Vanneman, Ellen Ruth Walker, Judy Walker, Kathleen Walters, Judy Warr, Vicki Weber, Charles Whitman, Branda Winans, Carol Ann Wisson.

spent five seasons in the singing ensemble and whose wife **Joanne** was in the 1961 ensemble, went on to become active in Christian TV in New York. **Steve Elmore**, ensemble member in 1953 and again in 1960-61, works in New York doing TV soap operas and commercials. Kansas Citian **Walter Hook**, who was in the Starlight singing ensemble for several seasons during the late '50s and early '60s, received the best actor award in Chicago in the mid-1980s for his role of the king in *The King and I* at the Candlelight Dinner Theatre. **James King**, ensemble member from Dodge City, Kansas, went on to sing at the Metropolitan Opera and was later knighted in Germany for his musical abilities.

Two former ensemble members are still touring the country. **Phil Rash** (1957-59) recently toured with *Oklahoma!* while **Fidel Romann** (known as Joaquin Romaguera) traveled with the cast of *Cats.* **Paul Haugh** (1966-67) appeared in the film *In Cold Blood* and is the current acting director at The Heartland Theatre in Kansas City.

Vivien Ferrara, daughter of Tony Ferrara and child performer on the Starlight stage, is now an actress/singer in Los Angeles. **Judith Blegen** became

a principal singer with the Metropolitan Opera in New York and has been seen on the Johnny Carson show.

Several of the Starlight performers became producers or directors of other theatrical projects. **Arthur Bartow**, who was in the ensemble in '56 and '57 and took supporting roles in '58, '59, '67, '68, '70, and '74, became a published author of a book about directors. **Robert Turoff**, a graduate of Central High School in Kansas City, Missouri, and then the University of Denver, served as assistant director in 1958 and 1959 under Glenn Jordan and Bert Yarborough. He became the producer of The Golden Apple, a dinner theatre in Sarasota, Florida, during the 1970s, '80s and early '90s. **Mary Jo Grubach** (now known as Joelle Jons), ensemble member in 1959-60, has performed numerous roles at that theatre. **Michael P. Price**, who was the lighting director for Starlight in 1962, is presently the producer at Goodspeed Opera Company in Connecticut. **Jack Eddleman**, performer at Starlight in 1952-'53 and '56, was one of the directors for the Kansas City Lyric Opera.

The 1989 president of Metro-Goldwyn-Mayer/United Artists got his initiation into show business as a stagehand at Starlight. The fact that his last name was **Berger** did not keep **Rick** from working on the prop crew, loading lumber and, in general, learning the theatre business from the ground up as his father had done before him.

Many of Starlight's dancers have ventured successfully into professional careers. **Sandahl Bergman**, a member of the dancing ensemble during 1963-69, later went on to perform in *A Chorus Line* on Broadway and the movie *All That Jazz*. After four years in the ensemble, **Kathy Bartosh** and **Vicki Allen** left Starlight in 1969 and joined the Broadway production of *Coco*, which starred Katharine Hepburn and was choreographed by Michael Bennett. Kathy's husband, **Dennis Landsman**, also danced at Starlight. They now own the American Dance Center in Kansas City.

Elizabeth Kelley, a member of the ensemble in 1969, danced with the Dean Martin Show as a Goldigger. She is the director of Dance Studio I in Kansas City.

After his Starlight performances, **Steve Short** became a Folies Bergére dancer at the Las Vegas Tropicana Hotel. He also performed on the Carol Burnett TV series,

PHOTO COURTESY OF STARLIGHT THEATRE

Ian Sullivan, Dean Dittmann, Vester Swingle in *My Fair Lady*, 1964.

Above: **Billy Boy Smith**, *By the Beautiful Sea,* 1957. (Real name: Wilburn James Smith.)

Below: **Staging director** Glenn Jordan giving directions to "the lost boys" in *Peter Pan,* 1956.

danced in *Irene* and *Lorelei* on Broadway, and worked with Lucille Ball in the movie *Mame.* **Cheryl Clark**, a former dance ensemble member from 1962-71, later toured Europe with the Jim Nabors show.

Scott Barnard, who danced with the ensemble during 1965-67, became the assistant director of the Joffrey Ballet. **Katharine Plavcan** went on to head the dance department at the University of Missouri at Kansas City.

Orrin Kayan was a dance ensemble member in 1959 and 1963. His brother **Neal** conducted the Ruth Page Opera Ballet in Chicago. Neal came to Starlight in 1969 as assistant musical director, and Orrin went on to dance with the National Ballet in Washington, D.C.

Larry Long, who took his first job out of New York at Starlight, now heads the Ruth Page Foundation in Chicago. He has been the Ballet Master for the Lyric Opera of Chicago, a guest teacher of the Royal Swedish Ballet, and a guest teacher in Holland, New Zealand, England, Portugal, and Spain. His wife, the former **Delores Lipinski**, successfully auditioned for Starlight in Chicago in 1956. She teaches at the Ruth Page School of Dance in Chicago, as does **Patricia Klekovic**, a Chicago-born featured dancer at Starlight from 1955-60.

John McFall, who at the age of fourteen was an extra in one of Starlight's large production numbers and then was in the ensemble in 1964, is the ballet master for the Ballet Metropolitan in Columbus, Ohio, the position he held formerly with the San Francisco Ballet. He also choreographed a ballet for Mikhail Baryshnikov for the American Dance Theatre.

Starlight Theatre was a training ground and master teacher to many of these talented people. The theatre provided an opportunity to create, to develop, and to survive as a young performer. The intensity of the work proved their mettle. **Larry Long** stated, "The experience of Starlight taught many a young performer his stagecraft, his professionalism, his dedication. Starlight was a tremendous learning experience because so much work had to be done in so little time in such concentrated fashion. It was a laboratory for learning one's trade."

When young talent came to Starlight, they knew they were starting at the top as far as summer stock was concerned. The Muny and Starlight were considered the "plums" of summer work. When young performers came to the Kansas City theatre, they realized they were fortunate to have a long season and the opportunity to take part in a grand production Broadway style—not an abbreviated version done with six dancers on some small stage somewhere. In the 1950s and '60s, Starlight had a resident dance company of fourteen women and seven men, a resident singing ensemble of twenty-four singers, and a resident acting company. Larry Long continued: "It was top drawer experience and of a kind that was invaluable. Without one day off for all those weeks, the performers learned how to pace themselves, how to give when they needed to give, how to conserve, how to learn new material, and how to retain it. They learned so much from watching professionals like Joe Macaulay, Dean Ryan, Tony Ferrara. They learned so much."

Vicki Allen, who after dancing on Broadway went on to work with Tony Bennett on his nightclub circuit, to choreograph for opera companies and summer stock, and to work as assistant for the Kansas City Ballet Company, reminisced,

> *You spent so much time there that it was like home. You lived there. It was a wonderful way to grow up in the theatre. Dancers learned to sing, you knew all the words to the songs, singers learned to dance. You were like a little mouse in the corner watching it all. You saw the orchestra rehearse, you watched the sound men adjust the mikes, you watched the light men plotting the light cues. In the costume shop you heard people complaining, "It's the wrong color, it's too long, it's too tight, she can't sing in it." You weren't there just being a dancer. That's where I learned theatre. You were surrounded by professionals all the way—living and breathing theatre.*

According to **Steve Short**, the present owner and director of the Kansas City Costume Company who graduated from Pembroke Country Day High School and spent two seasons on the Starlight stage,

> *Starlight was our Peanuts security blanket. Later in my professional career when I had to dance all day and perform all night and others in the cast were complaining about the work, I was prepared because it was nothing compared to what we did at Starlight. When Tommy Tune came to Starlight and choreographed* State Fair *in 1969 with the original choreography from Broadway, I remember the dancers lying in the wings gasping for breath, the routine was so difficult. But we did it! We had received superior training in technique at the Conservatory; but Starlight stretched us—pushed us to the edge of our endurance, made us learn musical comedy routines, a lighter style of dance than we were accustomed to, and forced us to project beyond the footlights. When I was working on the movie* Mame *with Lucille Ball in the early 1970s, I was amazed that six of the dancers in that show had been at Starlight. My only regret was that I didn't go there sooner. Starlight was the great catalyst in my life.*

PHOTOS COURTESY OF STARLIGHT THEATRE

Top: **Patricia Klekovic** and Orrin Kayan.

Below: **Irwin Charone**, the second most frequently seen character actor on the Starlight stage, with Ann Blyth in *The Merry Widow*, 1969.

VARIOUS CHILDREN'S CHORUSES OF THE 1950s

Children's chorus: *Damn Yankees*, 1957. *Left to right, front row:* Diane Murry, Kay Butler, Chrissie Ferguson, Patty Merryman. *Second row groupings:* Monica Renwick, Jill Hait, Susie Pearson, Sue Hunziker, Debbie Duff, Nanci Bergman, Debbie Riggs, Vida Rickert, Stephanie McMay. *Third row:* Debbie Hallek, Susie Scott, Judy Williams. *Back row:* Vickie Ellis, Sandra Slenker, Myra Jean Simpson, Debbie Weaver, Melissa Stoneburn, Sandahl Bergman, Susie Wolzak, and Gretchen White.

Children's chorus: *The King and I*, 1956. *Left to right, front row:* Susan Shigemura, Steve Kanagawa, Christine Kanagawa, Rose Marie Florez, and Ginger Sue Tanaka. *Center row:* Julia Alvarez, Win Odo, Robert Chavez, Lyle Odo, Beatrice Muzquiz, and Patricia Muzquiz. *Back row:* Peggy Seo, Gregory Ono, Alan Tanaka, Harold Tuck, Ronald Kanagawa, and Sandra Odo.

THE STORY OF STARLIGHT THEATRE

Boys Chorus for *Carmen*, 1954.
Sixth row left to right: Donald Bell, Steve Eckles, and Mickey Cooper.
Fifth row: Richard Jorgensen, Peter McQueeny, and Kevin Onka.
Fourth row: Albert Mosqueda, Randy Grimm, and James Douglas
Edwards. *Third row:* Billie Protys, Fred Huff, and James Tarwater.
Second row: Pat Lynch, Tommy Beets, and John Adams. *First row:*
Eugene Richmond, Morris Glynn, and Roy Kline. Absent from picture:
Harry Hopper.

Children's choreographer Virginia
Loncar with children's chorus of *The
Red Mill*, 1952.
Front row left to right: Sharon Wiber,
Linda Douglas, Madelyn Voigts,
Susan Bras, Julianne Loncar,
Wanda Zackert, Betty Moller, Carol
Kindell, Kathleen Hegarty. *Second
row left to right:* Sue Ellen Starkey,
Kathy Hall, Paula Illmer, Judy
Moore, Judith Ann Nastav, Judy
Ricard, Patty Martin, Peggy
Tarwater, Lanie Ebert, Glenda
Holdner. *Back row left to right:*
Sharon Kelley, Diane Huston,
Roberta Holt, Monica Doohan, Billie
Ann Bernardel, Patty Bova, Carol
Fessler, Judy Cole, and children's
choreographer Virginia Loncar.

Elaine Loughead *(center)* with Patti Parla, Jeanie Meroney and Vicki Joseph.

Another veteran performer who came to Starlight and graduated to other adventures was **Tatiana Dokoudovoska**. She had auditioned in New York for Richard Berger after having performed for years with the American Ballet Theatre and the Ballet Russe de Monte Carlo. At the audition, she excused herself from the tap dancing section. "I can't dance like that," she pleaded with Berger as she tried to leave. But Berger stood in the doorway of the audition hall and stated, "I'm not going to let you go." When she arrived at the Kansas City theatre, a television interview featuring Starlight dancers brought her to the attention of Wiktor Labunski, the Director of the Conservatory of Dance. He asked her to come and teach. She was an instructor at the Conservatory from 1954 until she retired in July of 1989. She was partly responsible for the superb training of many young dancers who later came to Starlight.

Actors, too, found the Starlight experience a real test of their abilities. **Arthur Bartow**, who became a director and producer in New York, stated, "The strength of a stage like Starlight lies in spectaculars on a heroic scale. In summer stock like Starlight, the actor had to sell himself to the audience, make immediate contact and leave something with each person. You had to deliver."

Irwin Charone, a veteran actor before he came to Kansas City in 1964, played thirty-three different roles on the Starlight stage. He recounted twenty-six years later, "All I had ever learned about voice projection, diction, how to use body language for comic effect—all that came into being when I had to appear on that huge stage. I look back on those days with great memories."

Even those young talents who did not go on to performance careers found the experience of Starlight important to their lives. **Elaine Loughead**, the former dance captain of the Starlight company, got her first taste of live theatre when she accompanied her neighbor to the 1956 Starlight production of *Peter Pan*. Three decades later she still remembers her first thoughts: "I went out of the theatre gates determined that I would get into theatre and particularly Starlight." As circumstances worked out, she danced there for many seasons. At age fourteen (she lied about her age) she joined the ensemble and stayed at Starlight for nearly ten years, becoming one of the first women on Dick Berger's production staff. She recounts, "Starlight taught discipline, responsibility, and courage—the courage to set other goals and reach them."

Victoria Sherry, wife of conductor Roland Fiore and herself a frequent leading lady at Starlight, is the producer of an opera company in Philadelphia. In a 1990 production of the ballad opera *The Horse of Credulity*, she was faced with the problem of how to move the scenes along within the confines of the small Walnut Theatre. Her own experience of performing on the Starlight stage reminded her of how the islands on each side of the stage were lit in order to portray a short intimate scene while the main stage was being set for larger production numbers. Sherry testified that "all the planning which went into the pacing and the locations of the sets for the Philadelphia opera production were a direct result of being at Starlight."

Katie Madden was a fresh Loretto Academy graduate when her drama teacher escorted her to a Starlight audition. She wasn't cast that year, but four years later she did receive the nod from Berger and spent two seasons at the theatre. Having been thoroughly trained by her high school theatre coach, **Sister Ancella Marie**, Katie was an instant success with Berger who found she could memorize a script overnight. He used the threat of an eager and competent understudy against many a leading lady. The threat turned into a reality during the 1964 season when Helena Bliss became ill and Katie had to take over the lead role in *Milk and Honey*. When questioned about her recollections of opening night, Katie stated, "It was the most natural thing in the world to appear on that stage. When I was a little girl, I would occasionally get to go with my uncle who had season tickets at Starlight. I use to fantasize about being a star on that stage. The idea had been incubating within me for years before it actually happened. When opening night did come and I did appear in a lead role, it was no surprise." When asked what impressions she took with her from having performed for two seasons at the theatre, she said, "My experience at Starlight taught me that the best people in the profession are genuine and good people. They are approachable and helpful to other aspiring actors. I learned a tolerance and appreciation for people"—an attitude she carried with her into other walks of life.

The present director of the Wichita Children's Theatre is a former child performer at Starlight. **Monica Doohan Flynn** made her debut in the 1951 *Babes in Toyland* and continued to perform in the children's shows of 1952 (*The Red Mill*) and 1953 (*The Wizard of Oz*). She also starred as one of Annie's sisters in the 1953 and 1956 productions of *Annie Get Your Gun*. In 1990, looking back on her performing years, Flynn reminisced, "Starlight whetted my appetite for theatre. Had it not been for Starlight, I would not have been exposed to professional theatre. The interaction with other actors and directors provided me with a much more professional atmosphere. I carry that with me today."

These recollections are a sampling of stories by adults who found that their experience as a youth at Starlight Theatre helped them to learn lessons which they later applied to other facets of life. The theatre taught many young Kansas Citians about their abilities, the workings of a professional theatre, the challenges of life, and the importance of kindness and encouragement to others. Starlight Theatre was indeed a training ground for a wide variety of life experiences.

Annie Get Your Gun, 1953. *Center:* Mark Reveaux, son of Edward Reveaux, staging director; *back row, left to right:* Julianne Loncar, Monica Doohan, Juliana Doohan, and Sharon Feigenbaum.

PHOTO COURTESY OF JOHN DOOHAN

Sigmund Romberg, one of the fathers of the American operetta, holds a special place in Kansas City theatre history. On opening night, June 25, 1951, he mounted the podium at Starlight Theatre, lifted his baton, and signaled the beginning notes of his *The Desert Song*. This moment of glory lasted only the few minutes it took the musicians to play the overture; Romberg then handed the conductor's baton to Roland Fiore and left the remainder of the evening's tunes to the Kansas City experts. Five months later, he died. The music and the style that he helped create for the American musical audience lasted a few short years after his passing.

Eight years earlier, Richard Rogers and Oscar Hammerstein II had composed their first smash hit, *Oklahoma!* Their collaboration perfected the musical play, and their first success was followed by *Carousel* (1945), *South Pacific* (1949), *The King and I* (1951), *The Sound of Music* (1959), and other lesser known works.

Years before their partnership, another twosome had written the songs for a book made into a play then into a movie. Harold Arlen, creator of "Stormy Weather" and "Blues in the Night," joined with E. Y. Harburg to write "We're Off to See the Wizard" and "Somewhere Over the Rainbow" for Frank Baum's book, *The Wizard of Oz*. Although the book was written in 1900, the musical has retained its appeal throughout the century. The 1991 production drew the largest audience of any show in Starlight's history (see the Starlight Awards on p.107).

Due to the sudden death of Jerome Kern who was scheduled to write the score, Oscar Hammerstein decided to ask Irving Berlin to try his luck with a book show. The result was *Annie Get Your Gun* (1946). Rogers and Hammerstein produced that show; Josh Logan was the staging director. A year later, *Brigadoon*, a fantasy musical, written by another famous team, Alan Jay Lerner and Frederick Loewe, opened in New York. Ten years later Jerome Robbins got his chance to add to American musical theatre history by choreographing a production in which dance was the primary means of storytelling—*West Side Story*, 1957. In that same year, Meredith Willson wrote a homespun story of a con artist visiting small Midwestern communities and selling them on the idea of a town band, *The Music Man*. And preceding all these shows, standing alone and serving as a beacon to illuminate the path, was Hammerstein and Kern's classic production *Show Boat* (1927).

PHOTO COURTESY OF TROY THOMAS PHOTOGRAPHY

Left to right: Carl DiCapo, Mrs. Clyde Nichols, Jr. (Martha), former president of the Starlight Association, and Mrs. Barnett C. Helzberg, Jr. (Shirley), present head of the Starlight Board.

All these productions were significant and marked, in some way, a milestone on the road to development of the American musical. These same productions served as milestones in Starlight's development as the showplace for musical theatre. It is no accident that all, except *Carousel*, have played Starlight five or six times as of 1992; *Carousel* has appeared four times, as have twelve other musicals (see the Production Frequency on p.121). But consider their Broadway birth dates—the "youngest" production is over thirty years old! Shows like these are not being produced currently in New York in the numbers seen in the '30s, '40s, and '50s. And this bit of information bears directly on the accumulating history of Starlight, for without new shows, the theatre's offerings must change. The ten productions a season that Richard Berger's staff provided in 1951 simply are not possible in the 1990s because of the decrease in new material being written for the New York stage.

Perhaps the prohibitive expense of mounting a Broadway production deters all but a few who venture to gamble. Perhaps the music writers who once frequented Tin Pan Alley in New York are elsewhere composing for television or music videos. Perhaps the taste of the American theatregoer has changed greatly, and the younger set raised on *Star Wars* and electronic music is not content to support the entertainment its parents found pleasing. Perhaps a hundred other reasons explain why the face of Broadway has changed, but the change is irrefutable. Time has aged the reproductive ability of the American musical. The young, the vigorous, the ever expanding outpouring of productions in the '30s, '40s, and '50s has slowed to a trickle, and because of that reduced flow, Starlight has had to look in the mirror, ponder what it perceives as an altered image, put on makeup, change the agenda, and go forth to greet a new generation of suitors.

Intimate shows with small casts don't play well on the big Starlight stage. Irving Berlin once remarked that he never wrote a bad song for Ethel Merman because he knew it would be heard in the last row. Starlight was built for that kind of boldness, power and spectacle; grand productions launched Starlight and earned its reputation as one of the country's leading outdoor theatres.

In recent summers Starlight has presented a combination of book musicals and concerts during its season. The theatre will continue to offer a variety of entertainment selections. The present and past presidents of the Board of Directors, Mrs. Barnett Helzberg, Jr. and Mrs. Clyde Nichols, Jr., along with the current general manager Robert Rohlf, and the vigilant Starlight Board, are absolutely devoted to the continuation of the theatre as a viable source of entertainment for Kansas Citians. These long range thinkers constantly investigate new avenues to interest a broader range of people, a younger generation, a new type of audience.

For over forty years now Starlight has been a landmark. Like the Plaza, the Liberty Memorial, and more recently Crown Center, Starlight has become a Kansas City institution, a unique facility offering a very different kind of theatre encounter that people in other American cities do not have the privilege of enjoying. Henry Haskell, in an article in *The Kansas City Star*, described the Starlight experience: "...it embraces the

An aerial view of Starlight Theatre and its grounds, 1992.

beauty of the setting, the relaxation of the outdoors, the informality of the procedure and, above all, the attribute of sociability. The friendliness of the audience of which you are a part at Starlight is one of the theatre's great charms."

Starlight Theatre is a magic place. An evening at the Swope Park theatre is an evening unlike any other. You sit under the stars, sometimes under the rain clouds, and become part of the process of creating. But the Delk-designed buildings provide only a background for the artistic experience. The play and the people are the heart of the matter.

The plays vary. Seventy productions have been seen on the big stage two or more times. Numerous others have appeared only once. The people change. The Starlight audience has always been a mix of rich and poor, young and old, couples and groups, families and friends, theatre buffs and novices. The patrons have come from offices and fields, grade schools and retirement homes, downtown and out-of-town, inner-city and suburb, the United States and foreign lands.

As the decades have passed, the plays and the audience members have changed, but the ultimate experience of outdoor theatre has not. On the hillsides of ancient Greece our theatrical forefathers laughed and cried, listened and learned, pondered and heeded. Twenty-three centuries later, the Starlight Theatre audiences continue to do the same. They hum along, enjoy the breeze, laugh at the frolic, delight in the dance, marvel at the spectacle, and are touched by the message. They continue to file out through the gates at the end of an evening's performance enriched and enlightened by their experience at the great amphitheatre nestled in Swope Park's rolling hills located eight miles south of the confluence of the two mighty rivers from which the city takes its name.

Finale

★ AWARDS ★

1951–1991

HIGHEST WEEKLY ATTENDANCE FOR A BOOK MUSICAL: *The Wizard of Oz*, 1991, (55,364).

HIGHEST WEEKLY ATTENDANCE FOR A VARIETY SHOW: *The Carol Burnett Show*, 1962, (55,142).

MOST PERFORMANCES BY A MALE: Joseph Macaulay, resident character actor from 1951-1963 who played the original role of Aramis on Broadway in Friml's *The Three Musketeers* (approximately 80 different roles).

   •HONORABLE MENTION: Irwin Charone, resident actor from 1964-1971, (33 different roles).

MOST PERFORMANCES BY A FEMALE: Lilian Armijo, Mrs. Jerry Funk, co-owner of Backstage Workshop in Kansas City (over 600 performances as a chorus member and supporting roles).

MOST LEAD PERFORMANCES BY A MALE: Donald Clarke.

MOST LEAD PERFORMANCES BY A FEMALE: Dorothy Coulter, Mrs. Joseph B. Hall, of Leawood, Kansas.

BEST DRESSED: Richard Berger (Always).

OLDEST STARLIGHT EMPLOYEE: James Craig, stagehand and first property master, age 85.

   •HONORABLE MENTION: Edward Maier, stagecrew, age 81.

MOST YEARS EMPLOYED: David Miller, head spotlight operator, 1951-1986 (two years not employed at Starlight), a total of 33 years.

   •HONORABLE MENTION: Al Krikorian, property master from 1962-1988, a total of 31 years (1957-1988).

LONGEST FAMILY DYNASTIES: The Obermeyers and the Millers.
   The Obermeyers. Father Herb as stagehand and second master carpenter, 1951-1974, son Burt 1965-present as Master Electrician, and Grandsons: Dale, Danny, Larry, Duane and Eric as stagehands and spotlight operators.
   The Millers. Father David, 1951-1986 (2 year vacation), head spotlight operator, sons Dave and John as ushers and spotlight operators.

THE QUIETEST OPENING NIGHT: Monday Aug. 14, 1989 (the traveling troupe of *Fiddler on the Roof* did not arrive in time to perform).

TOP TWO DOZEN MUSICALS 1951–1991:

1. *The Wizard of Oz*, 1991, (55,364)
2. *The Sound of Music*, 1977, (52,384)
3. *South Pacific*, 1991, (51,102)
4. *The King and I*, 1976, (50,565)
5. *A Chorus Line*, 1991, (50,404)
6. *Tom Sawyer*, 1964, (49,131)
7. *Bye Bye Birdie*, 1966, (48,323)
8. *West Side Story*, 1965, (48,076)
9. *West Side Story*, 1990, (47,849)
10. *The Sound of Music*, 1988, (47,829)
11. *Grease*, 1981, (47,510)
12. *South Pacific*, 1963, (47,251)
13. *My Fair Lady*, 1991, (46,858)
14. *Calamity Jane*, 1961, (46,733)
15. *Naughty Marietta*, 1951, (53,319 for eight nights. Prorated for seven nights, (46,654)
16. *Fiddler on the Roof*, 1989, (46,577) for only 6 nights
17. *The Unsinkable Molly Brown*, 1963, (46,457)
18. *Hello, Dolly!*, 1977, (46,195)
19. *Annie Get Your Gun*, 1956, (46,053)
20. *South Pacific*, 1955, (45,865)
21. *Mr. President*, 1964, (45,592)
22. *The Chocolate Soldier*, 1951, (45,426)
23. *Oklahoma!*, 1990, (45,055)
24. *Show Boat*, 1976, (44,995)

TOP FIVE VARIETY SHOWS:

1. *The Carol Burnett Show*, 1962, (55,142)
2. *The Jim Nabors Show*, 1971, (52,545)
3. *The Jim Nabors Show*, 1972, (46,792)
4. *The Concert Sound of Henry Mancini*, 1973, (44,892)
5. *Doc Severinsen*, 1973, (41,496)

★ SHOW CHRONOLOGY ★

1951

The Desert Song	Victoria Sherry-Brian Sullivan-Donald Clarke	June 25-July 1
Rio Rita	Terry Saunders-Donald Clarke	July 2-8
Song of Norway	Helena Bliss-John Tyers	July 9-15
Roberta	Terry Saunders-Biff McGuire	July 16-22
Rose Marie	Terry Saunders-John Tyers	July 23-29
The Chocolate Soldier	Helena Bliss-John Tyers-Billy Gilbert	July 30-Aug. 5
Brigadoon	Gloria Hamilton-John Tyers	Aug. 6-12
Bittersweet	Helena Bliss-Glenn Burris	Aug. 13-19
Babes in Toyland	Gloria Hamilton-Earl Williams-Gil Lamb	Aug. 20-26
Naughty Marietta	Rosemarie Brancato-Donald Clarke	Aug. 27-Sept. 3

1952

The Great Waltz	Brenda Lewis-Glenn Burris-Lillian Murphy	June 23-29
Good News	Bibi Osterwald-Jack Goode-Evelyn Wyckoff	June 30-July 6
The Vagabond King	Victoria Sherry-Edward Roecker	July 7-13
Where's Charley?	Marie Foster-Hal LeRoy-Byron Palmer	July 14-20
The Firefly	Rosemarie Brancato-Donald Clarke	July 21-27
Carousel	Gloria Hamilton-Edward Roecker	July 28-Aug. 3
Robin Hood	Elaine Malbin-Donald Clarke-R. Wentworth	Aug. 4-10
East Wind	Victoria Sherry-Edward Roecker	Aug. 11-17
The Red Mill	Betty Ann Busch-Hal LeRoy-Paul Gilbert	Aug. 18-24
Show Boat	Gloria Hamilton-Donald Clarke-Sammy White	Aug. 25-Sept. 6

1953

The Student Prince	Lillian Murphy-Billy Gilbert-Glenn Burris	June 22-28
The Wizard of Oz	Jo Sullivan-Lou Seiler-Jack Eddleman	June 29-July 5
The Merry Widow	Jean Fenn-Ralph Herbert	July 6-12
Bloomer Girl	Kyle MacDonnell-Jim Hawthorne	July 13-19
On Your Toes	Pauline Deniston-Roy McDonald	July 20-26
Up in Central Park	Betty Ann Busch-Richard Atkinson	July 27-Aug. 2
The New Moon	Victoria Sherry-Walter Cassel	Aug. 3-9
Kiss Me Kate	Helena Bliss- John Tyers	Aug. 10-16
Blossom Time	Lillian Murphy-Walter Cassel-Helena Bliss	Aug. 17-23
Annie Get Your Gun	Janis Paige-William Shriner	Aug. 24-Sept. 6

1954

Call Me Madam	Billie Worth-Donald Burr	June 18-27
Sweethearts	Rowena Rollins-Joey Faye	June 28-July 4
The Three Musketeers	Victoria Sherry-Andrew Gainey	July 5-11
Girl Crazy	Betty O'Neil-Earl Williams	July 12-18
*Carmen**	Jean Madeira-Donald Clarke-Wm. Shriner	July 19-25
Gentlemen Prefer Blondes	Penny Singleton-Donald Burr	July 26-Aug. 1
Hit the Deck	Betty Ann Busch-Sterling Holloway	Aug. 2-8
Song of Norway	Lillian Murphy-Larry Brooks-Frances Greer	Aug. 9-15
No No Nanette	Ann Crowley-Romo Vincent	Aug. 16-22
Oklahoma!	Ann Crowley-Jim Hawthorne	Aug. 23-Sept. 5

*First opera

1955

Naughty Marietta	Rosemarie Brancato-Jim Hawthorne	June 20-26
Me and Juliet	Dorothy Coulter-Russell Arms	June 27-July 3
Babes in Toyland	Paula Stewart-John Henson-K. Albertson	July 4-10
Guys and Dolls	Penny Singleton-Mitchell Gregg-D. Coulter	July 11-17
Bittersweet	Jean Fenn-Robert Rounseville	July 18-24
Finian's Rainbow	Jo Sullivan-Don Beddoe	July 25-31
Cole Porter Festival	Victoria Sherry-Hal LeRoy-Betty O'Neil	Aug. 1-7
Brigadoon	Lillian Murphy-Robert Smith-Chris Robinson	Aug. 8-14
Wonderful Town	Helena Bliss-Chris Robinson-Betty Gillett	Aug. 15-21
South Pacific	Jeanne Bal-Webb Tilton-Jim Hawthorne	Aug. 22-Sept. 4

1956

Peter Pan	Jeanne Bal-Eric Brotherson	June 18-24
Kismet	Dorothy Coulter-Earle McVeigh-Marilyn Ross	June 25-July 1
Best Foot Forward	Penny Singleton-Peter Conlow-Barbara Cook	July 2-8
The Desert Song	Janet Medlin-Jim Hawthorne	July 9-15
Annie Get Your Gun	Gisele MacKenzie-Edward Roecker	July 16-22
Plain and Fancy	Evelyn Page-Robert Smith	July 23-29
The Chocolate Soldier	Laurel Hurley-Mitchell Gregg-Donald Clarke	July 30-Aug. 5
Paint Your Wagon	Dorothy Coulter-Edwin Steffe-Mitchell Gregg	Aug. 6-12
Wish You Were Here	Dorothy Coulter-Arnold Stang	Aug. 13-19
The King and I	Jeanette MacDonald-Leonard Graves	Aug. 20-Sept. 2

1957

*Liberace**		June 17-23
South Pacific	Martha Wright-Howard Keel	June 24-July 7
High Button Shoes	Jill Corey-Paul Gilbert-Hal LeRoy	July 8-14
Can Can	Hildegarde-John Tyers	July 15-21

110

By the Beautiful Sea	Lillian Roth-Webb Tilton	July 22-28
The Pajama Game	Fran Warren-Don Cornell	July 29-Aug. 4
Panama Hattie	Julie Wilson-Paul Lynde	Aug. 5-11
Silk Stockings	Julie Wilson-Tony Bennett	Aug. 12-18
Damn Yankees	Gretchen Wyler-Gale Gordon	Aug. 19-25
Show Boat	Dorothy Collins-Robert Rounseville	Aug. 26-Sept. 8
* First Variety Show		

1958

The Jerry Lewis Show		June 9-15
Fanny	Jan McArt-Wilbur Evans	June 16-22
Happy Hunting	Jane Kean-Bill Hayes	June 23-29
Rosalinda	Jean Fenn-Jack Russell	June 30-July 6
Kiss Me Kate	Janet Medlin-Julius LaRosa-Jane Kean	July 7-13
*Tom Sawyer**	Virginia Gibson-Randy Sparks	July 14-20
Carousel	Jan Clayton-Art Lund	July 21-27
The Wizard of Oz	Pat Suzuki-Leo DeLyon	July 28-Aug. 3
Guys and Dolls	Fran Warren-Frankie Laine-Romo Vincent	Aug. 4-17
The Most Happy Fella	Jan McArt-Robert Weede-Art Lund	Aug. 18-31
* World Premiere		

1959

Oklahoma!	Gogi Grant-Bill Hayes	June 15-21
The Firefly	Anna Maria Alberghetti-William McHale	June 22-28
Gentlemen Prefer Blondes	Barbara Heller-Iva Withers	June 29-July 5
Tom Sawyer	Randy Sparks-Virginia Gibson	July 6-12
Say, Darling	Johnny Desmond-Eddie Bracken-Jane Kean	July 13-19
The New Moon	Jan McArt-Earl Wrightson	July 20-26
The Great Waltz	Vic Damone-Clara Mae Turner	July 27-Aug. 2
The Bells Are Ringing	Sheila & Gordon MacRae-Charles Nelson Reilly	Aug. 3-16
Li'l Abner	Wynne Miller-Stuart Damon	Aug. 17-30

1960

Rose Marie	Anna Maria Alberghetti	June 20-26
Kismet	Dorothy Coulter-Earle McVeigh	June 27-July 3
Annie Get Your Gun	Gordon and Sheila MacRae	July 4-17
The Pajama Game	Elizabeth Allen-John Raitt	July 18-24
The Student Prince	Monte Amundsen-Bill Hayes	July 25-31
The Merry Widow	Patrice Munsel-George Gaynes-Glenn Burris	Aug. 1-7
*West Side Story**	Lee Venora-Lester James	Aug. 8-14
Meet Me In St. Louis	Peggy King-Richard Armbruster	Aug. 15-21

The King and I	Gisele MacKenzie-Leonard Graves	Aug. 22-Sept. 4
* First Touring Show		

1961

Destry Rides Again	Elizabeth Allen-Dick Shawn	June 19-25
The Vagabond King	Earl Wrightson-Jean Fenn	June 26-July 2
Red Head	Don Cornell-Cathryn Damon	July 3-9
Cinderella	Carla Alberghetti-Tommy Ralls-Hal LeRoy	July 10-16
Calamity Jane	Carol Burnett	July 17-30
Can Can	Genevieve	July 31-Aug. 6
Damn Yankees	Gale Gordon-Devra Korwin	Aug. 7-13
Take Me Along	Dan Dailey-Gloria Hamilton	Aug. 14-20
Flower Drum Song	Fran Warren-Kevin Scott	Aug. 21-Sept. 3

1962

The Music Man	Forrest Tucker-Louise O'Brien	June 18-July 1
Blossom Time	Lila Page-William Walker-Jim Hawthorne	July 2-8
Carol Burnett Show		July 9-15
Mexican Holiday	Bill Dana-Ballet Popular de Mexico	July 16-22
Around the World in Eighty Days	Cyril Ritchard-Jan McArt-Dom de Luise	July 23-Aug. 5
Fiorello	Tom Bosley-Dody Goodman	Aug. 6-12
Brigadoon	Dorothy Coulter-Forrest Tucker	Aug. 13-19
Bye Bye Birdie	Chita Rivera-Brenda Lee-Richard Barclay	Aug. 20-Sept. 2

1963

Show Boat	Dorothy Coulter-Robert Horton	June 17-30
Wildcat	Martha Raye-George Wallace	July 1-7
Carnival	Al Hirt-Lee Venora-Stephen Douglass	July 8-21
Gypsy	Gisele MacKenzie-George Nader	July 22-Aug. 4
The Unsinkable Molly Brown	New Christy Minstrels-Karen Morrow	Aug. 5-11
The Wizard of Oz	Connie Stevens-Will B. Able-Dean Dittmann	Aug. 12-18
Victor Borge		Aug. 19-25
South Pacific	Giorgio Tozzi-Elizabeth Allen	Aug. 26-Sept. 1

1964

My Fair Lady	Dorothy Coulter-Michael Allinson	June 22-July 5
Milk and Honey	Molly Picon-Giorgio Tozzi- Helena Bliss	July 6-12
Tom Sawyer	Bobby Rydell-Martin Ross	July 13-19
Tovarich	Ginger Rogers-John Vivyan	July 20-Aug. 2
Mr. President	Allen Ludden-Betty White	Aug. 3-9
Little Me	Donald O'Connor-Paula Stewart	Aug. 10-16

Porgy and Bess	Cab Calloway	Aug. 17-23
The Sound of Music	Nancy Dussault-Webb Tilton	Aug. 24-Sept. 6

1965

Camelot	Pernell Roberts-John Davidson-Margot Moser	June 21-July 4
The Music Man	Bert Parks-Wynne Miller- Dom de Luise	July 5-18
Kiss Me Kate	Earl Wrightson-Lois Hunt-Richard France	July 19-25
West Side Story	Anna Maria Alberghetti-Lester James	July 26-Aug. 1
Here's Love	Gretchen Wyler-Tab Hunter	Aug. 2-8
110 in the Shade	Constance Towers-John Davidson	Aug. 9-15
She Loves Me	John Gary-Gaylea Byrne-Barbara Ruick	Aug. 16-22
Oliver!	Jules Munshin-Bernice Massi	Aug. 23-Sept. 5

1966

How to Succeed in Business Without Really Trying	Don Ameche-Hal England-Dean Dittmann	June 20-July 3
The Desert Song	Peter Palmer-Dorothy Coulter	July 4-10
Bye Bye Birdie	Gary Lewis-Elaine Dunn	July 11-17
The Bells Are Ringing	Allen Ludden-Betty White	July 18-24
Flower Drum Song	Cely Carrillo-Yin Sun-Larry Leung	July 25-31
Oklahoma!	Jack Jones-Linda Michele-Karen Morrow	Aug. 1-14
Guys and Dolls	Bert Parks-Gretchen Wyler	Aug. 15-21
The King and I	Gisele MacKenzie-William Chapman	Aug. 22-Sept. 4

1967

West Side Story	Anna Maria Alberghetti-David Holliday	June 19-25
Kismet	Gordon MacRae-Barbara Meister	June 26-July 2
My Fair Lady	Dorothy Coulter-Michael Allinson	July 3-16
On a Clear Day You Can See Forever	Shirley Jones-Bill Hayes	July 17-23
The Unsinkable Molly Brown	The Serendipity Singers-Karen Morrow	July 24-Aug. 6
Funny Girl	Marilyn Michaels-Molly Picon-Danny Carroll	Aug. 7-13
It's a Bird! It's a Plane! It's Superman!	Bob Holliday-Charles Nelson Reilly	Aug. 14-20
The Sound of Music	Patrice Munsel-Reid Shelton	Aug. 21-Sept. 3

1968

Carousel	John Davidson-Barbara Meister	June 17-23
The Pajama Game	Gail Martin-Bill Hayes-Elaine Dunn	June 24-30
The Music Man	Forrest Tucker-Marilyn Savage	July 1-14
Annie Get Your Gun	Kaye Stevens-Bruce Yarnell	July 15-28
Call Me Madam	Ethel Merman-Richard Eastham-Russell Nype	July 29-Aug. 4

Sweet Charity	Patti Karr-Peter Lombard	Aug. 5-11
Show Boat	Arthur Godfrey-Judith McCauley	Aug. 12-18
South Pacific	Vikki Carr-Adair McGowen	Aug. 19-Sept. 1

1969

*The Nashville Sound**	Tex Ritter-Farron Young-Dottie West	June 16-22
State Fair	Ozzie and Harriet Nelson	June 23-July 6
Can Can	Marilyn Maye	July 7-13
Peter Pan	Ruta Lee-Murray Matheson	July 14-20
George M!	Danny Meehan-Richard France-Kitty Sullivan	July 21-Aug. 3
Damn Yankees	Cyd Charisse-Jerry Lanning-Jack Goode	Aug. 4-10
The Merry Widow	Ann Blyth-David Rae Smith-Coley Worth	Aug. 11-17
Mame	Gretchen Wyler	Aug. 18-31

*First Country Western Variety Show

1970

*Paul Revere and the Raiders**		June 22-28
Hello Dolly!	Marilyn Maye-Max Showalter	June 29-July 12
Tom Sawyer	Browning Bryant-Danny Lockin-Darlene Carr	July 13-19
On a Clear Day You Can See Forever	John Cullum-Nancy Dussault	July 20-26
Man of La Mancha	Ed Ames-Natalie Costa-Earle MacVeigh	July 27-Aug. 9
How to Succeed in Business Without Really Trying	Robert Morse-Willard Waterman	Aug. 10-16
Fiddler on the Roof	Jerry Jarrett-Delores Wilson-Helen Verbit	Aug. 17-30
First Edition	Kenny Rogers-Merle Haggard	Aug. 31-Sept. 6

*First Rock and Roll Variety Show

1971

Sweet Charity	Juliet Prowse-Chelsea Brown-Pat Turner	June 21-27
Funny Girl	Marilyn Michaels-James Luisi	June 28-July 4
The Unsinkable Molly Brown	Barbara Eden-Jerry Lanning	July 5-18
70, Girls, 70	Nancy Andrews-Coley Worth-Gil Lamb	July 19-25
Cabaret	Joel Gray-Jacqueline Mayro	July 26-Aug. 8
Carol Channing Show	Hines, Hines and Dad	Aug. 9-15
Jim Nabors Show		Aug. 16-22
Two by Two	Milton Berle-Nancy Andrews	Aug. 23-Sept. 5

1972

Tennessee Ernie Ford Show		June 19-July 2
Ed Ames Show		July 3-16
Jim Nabors Show		July 17-23

Robert Goulet Show	Carol Lawrence	July 24-30
From Vienna With Love	Teresa Stich-Randall Karl Terkal	July 31-Aug. 6
Roy Clark Show		Aug. 7-13
Mexican Holiday		Aug. 14-27
Shirley Jones Show		Aug. 28-Sept. 3

1973

Roy Clark Show		June 18-July 1
Doc Severinsen Show	Marilyn Maye	July 2-8
Pearl Bailey Show		July 9-22
Untamed Land	Jimmie Rodgers-Chuck Connors	July 23-Aug. 5
Mitzi Gaynor Show		Aug. 6-12
Festival U.S.A.	Gordon MacRae	Aug. 13-19
Henry Mancini	The New Christy Minstrels	Aug. 20-26
Carol Lawrence Show		Aug. 27-Sept. 2

1974

Doc Severinsen Show	Frankie Avalon	June 17-23
Connie Stevens Show		June 24-30
Shirley Jones–Jack Cassidy Show		July 1-7
Abrasevic		July 8-14
Jerry Lewis Show	Peter Marshall	July 15-28
Man of La Mancha	Herschel Bernardi-Annette Cardona	July 29-Aug. 11
Dionne Warwicke Show	Roger Williams	Aug. 12-18
Steve Allen–Jayne Meadows Show		Aug. 19-Sept. 1

1975

Peter Marshall Show	The Mills Brothers	June 16-22
Roger Miller	Ed McMahon	June 23-29
Carousel	Ed Ames-Patti Davis	June 30-July 13
Mitzi Gaynor Show		July 14-20
Danny Thomas Show		July 21-Aug. 3
Eddie Fisher Show	Della Reese	Aug. 4-10
Henry Mancini Concert		Aug. 11-17
The Wizard of Oz	The Hudson Brothers-Margaret Hamilton	Aug. 18-24

1976

The Student Prince	Jack Gilford-Allan Jones	June 21-27
Gone With The Wind	Sherry Mathis-David Canary	June 28-July 4
Buck Owens Show		July 5-11
On the Town	The Hudson Brothers	July 12-18
Show Boat	Shirley Jones-Gale Gordon	July 19-25

Isaac Hayes and Dionne Warwicke		July 26-Aug. 1
Fiddler on the Roof	Jan Peerce	Aug. 2-8
Mame	Angela Lansbury	Aug. 9-15
The King and I	Yul Brynner-Constance Towers	Aug. 16-22
1776	Peter Graves-Howard Da Silva	Aug. 23-29

1977

The Merry Widow	Roberta Peters-Werner Klemperer	June 20-26
Bobby Goldsboro–Donna Fargo Concert		June 27-July 3
Finian's Rainbow	Paul Williams-Nancy Dussault-Ron Husmann	July 4-10
Shenandoah	Ed Ames	July 11-17
Hello, Dolly!	Carol Channing-Eddie Bracken	July 18-24
Anthony Newley–Bernadette Peters		July 25-31
Kismet	Len Cariou-Virginia Martin-George Rose	Aug. 1-7
The Sound of Music	Shirley Jones-H.M.Wynant-Sheila Smith	Aug. 8-14
Sweet Charity	Carol Lawrence-Ted Pritchard	Aug. 15-21
Porgy and Bess	Broadway Cast	Aug. 22-28

1978

The Music Man	Tony Randall	June 19-25
Zorba	Theodore Bikel	June 26-July 2
7 Brides for 7 Brothers	Jane Powell-Howard Keel	July 3-9
Henry Mancini	Jose Feliciano	July 10-16
Gypsy	Angela Lansbury	July 17-23
Oklahoma!	John McCook-Carol Wilcox-Stubby Kaye	July 24-30
Doc Severinsen Show	Linda Hopkins	July 31-Aug. 6
Man of La Mancha	Ed Ames	Aug. 7-13
Damn Yankees	Michele Lee-Vincent Price	Aug. 14-20
Chicago	Larry Kert-Penny Worth-Kirsten Childs	Aug. 21-27

1979

My Fair Lady	David Birney-Anita Gillette	June 18-24
Guys and Dolls	Abe Vigoda-Hugh O'Brian-Kathryn Crosby	June 25-July 1
Brigadoon	Jack McCook-Victoria Mallory	July 2-8
Blackstone Magic Show		July 9-15
A Funny Thing Happened on the Way to the Forum	Arte Johnson-Avery Schreiber	July 16-22
Sugar	Robert Morse-Ken Berry-Donald O'Connor	July 23-29
The Desert Song	Ann Blyth-Richard Fredricks	July 30-Aug. 5
I Do! I Do!	Howard Keel-Carol Lawrence	Aug. 6-12
Ballroom	Janis Paige-Forrest Tucker	Aug. 13-19
The Wiz	Deborah Malone-Ira Hawkins	Aug. 20-26

1980

Bubbling Brown Sugar	Cab Calloway	June 16-22
Anything Goes	Ginger Rogers-Sid Caesar	June 23-29
South Pacific	Florence Henderson-Giorgio Tozzi	June 30-July 6
Gabriel Kaplan–Vicki Carr		July 7-13
An Evening with Joel Grey and	*Peter Nero*	July 14-20
Bye Bye Birdie	Chita Rivera-Russ Tamblyn	July 21-27
Al Jolson Tonight	Larry Kert	July 28-Aug. 3
4 Girls 4	Rosemary Clooney-Rose Marie	
	Helen O'Connell-Margaret Whiting	Aug. 4-10
Li'l Abner	Joe Namath	Aug. 11-17
Jack Jones–Melissa Manchester Concert		Aug. 18-24

1981

Grease	Eddie Mekka-Andrea McArdle	July 6-12
Oliver!	Orson Bean-Heather McRae	July 20-26
Camelot	Noel Harrison-Anna Maria Alberghetti	Aug. 3-9
West Side Story	Barry Williams	Aug. 24-30

1982

The Sound of Music	Victoria Mallory-George Peppard	July 20-26
Where's Charley?	Robert Morse-Edie Adams	Aug. 10-16
The Best Little Whorehouse in Texas	Barbara Eden-Art Lund-Edwina Lewis	Aug. 24-30

1983

Ain't Misbehavin'	Demond Wilson-Debra Byrd	June 20-26
Annie	Peggy Cass-Harve Presnell	July 11-17
Fiddler on the Roof	Theodore Bikel-Thelma Lee	July 25-31
Man of La Mancha	David Holliday-Emily Yancy	Aug. 8-14
They're Playing Our Song	Anson Williams-Leslie Easterbrook	Aug. 22-28

1984

Cabaret	Bert Convy-D'Jamin Bartlett-Robert Clary	June 25-July 1
The Wizard of Oz	JoAnne Worley-Paul Williams	July 9-15
Annie Get Your Gun	Dee Wallace-John McCook	July 23-29
Jesus Christ Superstar	David Cassidy-Nicolette Larson	Aug. 6-12

1985

A Chorus Line	Donna McKechnie	June 24-30
Evita	Florence Lacy-R. Michael Baker	July 15-21

The Music Man	William Katt-Meg Bussert	July 29-Aug. 4
Hair	David Naughton	Aug. 12-18

1986

West Side Story	Stephen Lehew-Diane Fratantoni	June 23-29
Peter Pan	Lisa Whelchel	July 7-13
Sweet Charity	Georgia Engel-Lenny Wolpe	July 21-27
Dancin'		Aug. 4-10
Gentlemen Prefer Blondes	Morgan Fairchild	Aug. 18-24

1987

Gypsy	JoAnne Worley-Audrey Landers	June 8-14
Cinderella	Stephen Lehew	June 22-28
My One and Only	Georgia Engel	July 6-12
42nd Street		July 20-26
Big River and the Adventures of Huckleberry Finn	Romain Fruge-Michael Edward Stevens	Aug. 17-23

1988

*The Odd Couple**	Tim Conway-Tom Poston	June 20-26
The Sound of Music	Debby Boone	July 11-17
Jesus Christ Superstar	Stephen Lehew	July 25-31
Oliver!	Davy Jones	Aug. 8-14

*First Non-Musical Play

1989

Bye Bye Birdie	Gary Sandy	June 26-July 2
Annie	Mary-Pat Green-Danielle Findley	July 10-16
The King and I	Stacey Keach-Mary Beth Peil	July 24-30
Fiddler on the Roof	Topol-Marcia Rodd	Aug. 14-20

1990

Oklahoma!	John Davidson-Kim Crosby-Jamie Farr	June 25-July 1
Camelot	David Birney	July 9-15
West Side Story	Peter Gantenbein-Betsy True	July 23-29
Brigadoon	John Schneider-John James	Aug. 6-12

1991

A Chorus Line		June 24-30
My Fair Lady	Christina Andreas, John Neville, Clive Revill	July 8-14
The Wizard of Oz	Phyllis Diller	July 22-28
South Pacific	Harve Presnell-Alyson Reed	Aug. 5-11

1992

The Music Man	Gary Sandy	June 19-28
Peter Pan	David Ogden Stiers-B. D. Wong	July 3-12
Show Boat	Gavin MacLeod-Joel Higgins-Victoria Mallory	July 20-26
Hello, Dolly!	Madeline Kahn-John Schuck	Aug. 3-9

★ PRODUCTION FREQUENCY ★

1951–1992

SHOWS WHICH HAVE PLAYED SIX TIMES:

The Music Man
Show Boat
South Pacific
West Side Story
The Wizard of Oz

SHOWS WHICH HAVE PLAYED FIVE TIMES:

Annie Get Your Gun
Brigadoon
The King and I
Oklahoma!
The Sound of Music

SHOWS WHICH HAVE PLAYED FOUR TIMES:

Bye Bye Birdie
Carousel
The Desert Song
Damn Yankees
Fiddler on the Roof
Guys and Dolls
Kismet

Man of La Mancha
The Merry Widow
My Fair Lady
Peter Pan
Sweet Charity
Tom Sawyer

SHOWS WHICH HAVE PLAYED THREE TIMES:

Camelot
Can Can
Doc Severinsen
Gentlemen Prefer Blondes
Gypsy
Hello, Dolly!
Henry Mancini Concert

Kiss Me Kate
Oliver!
The Pajama Game
The Student Prince
The Unsinkable Molly Brown

SHOWS WHICH HAVE PLAYED TWO TIMES:

Annie
Babes in Toyland
The Bells are Ringing
Bittersweet
Blossom Time
Cabaret
Call Me Madam
Cinderella
The Chocolate Soldier
A Chorus Line
Roy Clark Show
Finian's Rainbow
Flower Drum Song
The Firefly
Funny Girl
Mitzi Gaynor Show
The Great Waltz
*How to Succeed in Business
 Without Really Trying*

Jesus Christ Superstar
Jack Jones Show
Shirley Jones Show
Jerry Lewis
Li'l Abner
Mame
Mexican Holiday
Jim Nabors Show
Naughty Marietta
The New Moon
*On a Clear Day You Can See
 Forever*
Porgy and Bess
Rose Marie
Song of Norway
The Vagabond King
Dionne Warwicke
Where's Charley?

PRODUCTION STAFF

PRODUCER DIRECTOR:
  Richard Berger 1951-1971

BUSINESS MANAGER:
  William Symon 1951-1965
  Anthony Ferrara 1965-1971

GENERAL MANAGER:
  Anthony Ferrara 1972-1980
  Alan McCracken 1981
  Robert Rohlf 1982-Present

RESIDENT STAGE DIRECTOR:
  Robert Ross 1951
  Edward Reveaux 1952-1953
  Glenn Jordan 1954-1958
  Bert Yarborough 1959-1962
  Glenn Jordan 1963-1966

RESIDENT ASSISTANT TO STAGE
DIRECTOR:
  Maury Tuckerman 1954-1955
  Walter Swift 1956
  Ed Sostek 1957
  Robert Turoff 1958-1959
  Maury Tuckerman 1960
  Richard Hughes 1961
  George W. Wasko, Jr. 1962-1970
  Douglas Gordon Matheson 1971

RESIDENT SCENIC DESIGNER:
  Albert Johnson 1951
  G. Philippe de Rosier 1952-1975

RESIDENT LIGHTING DESIGNER:
  Albert Johnson 1951
  G. Philippe de Rosier 1952-1975

RESIDENT STAGE MANAGER:
  Bill Ross, William Meader 1951
  Clem Egolf 1952
  William Meader 1953-1955
  Anthony Ferrara 1954
  Anthony Ferrara, Art Dilks 1955
  Anthony Ferrara 1956-1963
  Jerry Funk 1965-1968
  Bob Fahey 1969
  Michael Bradshaw 1970-1978
  Jerry Funk 1979-1980

RESIDENT ASSISTANT
STAGE MANAGERS:
  Anthony Ferrara 1951
  Anthony Ferrara, Morgan James 1952
  Anthony Ferrara,
    Maury Tuckerman 1953
  Maury Tuckerman 1954-1955
  Charles Murawski 1956-1958
  Jerry Funk 1959-1962
  Benjamin Siegler 1963
  Jonathon Chappell 1964
  Damon Weber 1965-1966

Allan Mitchell 1967
Bob Fahey 1968-1969
D. Richard Will 1970
G. J. Koellsted 1971-1972
Stuart Hale, Joe Watson 1976

RESIDENT MUSICAL DIRECTOR:
Roland Fiore 1951-1968
Dean Ryan 1969-1971

RESIDENT ASSOCIATE
MUSICAL DIRECTOR:
Harold Decker 1951
Sherman Frank 1952-1954
Rudolph Bennett 1955
Jack Lee 1956-1958
Alfred Heller 1959
Dean Ryan 1960-1968
Neal Kayan 1969
Dan Strickland 1970
Thomas Booth 1971

RESIDENT CHOREOGRAPHER:
Vonn Hamilton 1951
Theodore Adolphus 1952-1954
James Jamieson 1955-1957
Duncan Noble 1958
Harding Dorn 1959-1971

RESIDENT ENSEMBLE DIRECTOR:
Warren Boudinot 1951-1952
Diane Marsh 1953
William Holbrook 1954
Don Weissmuller 1955
Harding Dorn 1956-1958
Richard France and Ellen Ray 1959
Alex Palermo 1960
Ted Forlow 1961
Larry Long 1962-1964
Ralph McWilliams 1965
Buck Heller 1966
David Neuman 1967

Elaine Loughead 1968-1969
Dorothy Alfred 1970-1971

RESIDENT LIGHTING
COORDINATOR:
Danny Franks 1953
Donald La Mon, Al Burns 1954
Don Murphy 1955-1956
Carol Hoover 1957
John Cooper 1958
Norman Blumenfeld 1959
Lloyd Evans 1960-1961
Michael Price 1962
Marc Cohen 1963
Todd Glen 1964
Marc Cohen 1965
Richard Watkins 1966-1967
Ward Russell 1968
Richard Harden 1969
G. J. Koellsted 1970
Richard Watkins 1971-1976
David Ness 1977-1978
Bruce Rogers 1979-1980

REHEARSAL PIANIST:
Mrs. Louise Denham 1951
Pearl Roemer Kelly 1952
Veva A. Koenig 1953
Jane Ehart 1954-1956
Annette Story 1957-1971 1976-1978

MUSIC LIBRARIAN:
Lawrence Long 1951
Carl Douglass 1951-1980

TECHNICAL STAFF

MASTER CARPENTER:
  Ancel Lacy 1951-1963
  Herman Obermeyer 1964-1974
  Randy Halsey 1975-Present

MASTER PRODUCTION
CARPENTER:
  Walter Brown 1951-1953
  Robert Hennessy 1954-1970
  Frank Thomas 1971-1982
  Rick Gaskill 1983-1990
  Mark Stinner 1991
  Gil Vinzant 1992

MASTER ELECTRICIAN:
  H. G. Milligan 1951-1952
  Harold Childers 1953-1964
  Mike Hennessy 1965-1967
  David Hennessy 1968-1975
  Burt Obermeyer 1976-Present

BUILDING ELECTRICIAN:
  Floyd Finch 1971-1975
  Jerry Junkins 1976-1986
  Greg Brown 1992

PROPERTY MASTER:
  James Craig 1951-1952
  James Mace 1953-1955
  James Craig 1956-1957
  Charles LaMonica 1958-1961
  Al Krikorian 1962-1988
  Dave Lewis 1989-1992

MASTER ARTIFICER:
  James Craig 1951-1954
  Bill Brown 1955-1968
  Tim Hartnett 1969-1975
  Chuck Chaffee 1976-1981
  Pat Morris 1982-1992

MASTER SCENIC PAINTER:
  Emmett O'Connell 1951-1960
  Clive Rickabaugh 1961
  Paul Fanning 1962
  Richard Johnson 1963
  Robert Benstead 1964
  Gene Lee 1965
  John Rothgeb 1966
  Robert Benstead 1967-1979
  James Finger 1980
  Donna Slager 1982-1986
  Carl Kochvar 1987-1991
  Les Woods 1992

RESIDENT SOUND MAN:
  Carl Snow 1951-1957
  Ray Maier 1958-1980

RESIDENT WARDROBE MISTRESS:
  Virginia Donovan 1951-1963
  Ann Sheets 1964-1969
  Clara Louise Hall 1970-1980

★ STARLIGHT ASSN PRESIDENTS ★

1991-1992	Mrs. Barnett C. Helzberg, Jr. (Shirley)—Helzberg Diamonds
1988-1990	Mrs. Clyde Nichols, Jr. (Martha)—Civic Leader, *First Female President*
1986-1987	Mr. Robert Kipp—Hallmark Cards, Inc.
1983-1985	Jack Steadman—Kansas City Chiefs/Hunt Enterprises
1981-1982	W. W. Bennett—Bennett Construction Company
1980	Earnest Dick—Jack Henry Clothing Company
1978-1979	James T. Britt—Spencer, Fane, Britt & Brown
1976-1977	William T. Shields—*The Kansas City Star*
1974-1975	Clair H Schroeder—United Missouri Bank
1973	Davis K. Jackson—J. C. Nichols Company
1972	L. P. Cookingham—City Manager, City of Kansas City, Missouri
1970-1971	John Ayres—Cook Paint & Varnish Co.
1968-1969	George H. Clay—Federal Reserve Bank
1967	Marvin B. Marsh—Marsh Steel
1965-1966	Ralph L. Gray—Sheffield Steel
1963-1964	R. Carter Tucker—Gage & Tucker
1961-1962	Maurice Breyer—Harzfelds
1959-1960	J. F. Pritchard Jr.—Pritchard Corporation
1958	Paul Connor—Western Auto
1957	William E. Kemp—Kemp Koontz Claggett & Norquist
1956	Frank H. Spink—Bunting Hardware
1955	Henry Massman, Sr.—Massman Construction
1954	William N. Deramus—Kansas City Southern Industries
1953	Herbert H. Wilson—Emery, Bird, Thayer
1951-1952	John A. Moore—John A. Moore Realty Company

KANSAS CITY CENTENNIAL ASSOCIATION

Presents

"THRILLS OF A CENTURY"

A JOHN B. ROGERS PRODUCTION

Scenario By HERBERT O. BRAYER

STARLIGHT THEATRE

SWOPE PARK,   KANSAS CITY, MO.

JUNE 3 THRU JULY 5, 1950

NIGHT PERFORMANCES 8:15 P.M.

Production Staff

LEO SPAETH Managing Director	**JOHN W. JUDD** Producer	**PAUL T. HAAGEN** Technical Director
PAUL P. DOWNS Assistant Managing Director	**RITA M. HAAGEN** Director of Wardrobe	**JOHN J. VINCE** Choreographer & Assistant Producer

JAMES W. KLING, ARDEN PETING, WILLIAM HARFORD

Associate Technical Directors

SID EKDALE, JR. Director Second Cast	**JOHN FUHRMANN** Associate Director

STAGE CONSTRUCTION
Courtesy of Local Union Members, affiliated with the
Carpenters' District Council

"Miss Kansas City", Queen of the Centennial

MISS CLARA SMITH

Pages for the Queen: GAIL McMILLEN, VICKIE McBEATH

"Miss United States" . . . . . . **MISS JUANITA HUPPE**

Page for Miss U. S.: WILMA WEST

THE PRINCESSES

Misses Connie Caraway, Maxine Horner, Eunice Moore, Jean Maddox, Betty Bills, Joselyn De Shong, Betty Davidson, LaDell Hayes, Dorothy White, Joyce Schutte, Mary England, Karthryn Rosenburger, Lucy Wilson, Pat Hermann, Virginia R. Elliott, Norma Jean Robb, Betty Joan Baldus, Sally Butler, Nancy Rove, Barbara Coppinger, Shirley Sivils, Gloria Ashens, Ginger Bright, Earlene Danielsen, Rosemary Spiegelhalter, Edna Bryan, Virginia Scott, Jeanne Jones.

Prologue

"KANSAS CITY WELCOMES THE NATION"

Guards for Queen: Jan Turton, Phyllis Clark, Claudetta West, Norma Blacksmith, Donna Jasper, Barbara Hart, Janet Severin, Adele Nelson, Pat Mackey, Marilyn Whitehill, Dana Springer, Janet Wann, Marjorie Mackey, Sue Summerville, Alice Owens, Barbara Barnett, Judy Fincke, Judy Estell, Mary Lou Eklund, Sondra Phillips, Ester Laughlin, Dolores Dorney, Norma Norris

Men as Official Escorts:

The United States: Norma Glouiand, Barbara Jones, Claribel Rife, Dorothy Wheat, Helen Scott, Hortense Schaller, Virginia Clevenger, Nina Shively, Edith Devall, Lillian Mosby, Essie Millett, Olga Bennett, Mrs. Peter Pena, Leah Hart, Glenna Ellis, Leona Rider, Lula Maloney, Lucy Webb, Jean Warrell, Nina Molleson, Helen Clevenger, Kate Hacker, Ida Adamson, Maud Smart, Charline Michael, Maude Winkelman, Elizabeth Kohlmeyer, Ethelyn Joseph, Lucille Weaver, Myrtle Barber, Miriam Rowland, Harvey Ann Williamson, Bobby Brown, Marilyn Ferguson, Jane Halstead, DuAyne Eklund, Rosemary Sieve, Jayne Davis

U.S. Flag Bearers: Betty Winfrey, Pat Poulter, Carol Ray, Barbara Dickson, Nancy Griffith, Carol Russel, Claudia McReynolds, Sue Bates, Nancy Buger, Janice Blickhan, Leu Jones, Elizabeth Fassig, Barbara Jean Allard, Margaret Smalley, Jean Sorenson, Anne Rumsey, Carol Yoke, Jill Havener, Jane Bowersock, Joann Elliot, Irene Meek, Margarite Smith, Nancy Smith, Sylvia Smith, Mitzi Smith, Barbara Biurvall, Edna Robinson, Arlene Meek, Kathy Williams, Dunk Renwald, Sally Rendigs, Carolyn Harper, Nancy Britten, Pat Thies, Carol Reed, Mary Lawrence, Janice Shenk, Jeannie Grout, Diane Benedix, Marion McCoy, Barbara Avril, Jeannine Wilkerson, Lois Kasler, Nancy Burke, Barbara Anderson, Barbara Thompson, Iva Hoggatt, Marilyn Wycoff, Margaret Flanagan

Trumpeters: Patricia Hays, Lyle Mesker, Margaret Brown, Mary Louis Ross, Jan Cochran, Mary Ellen Cornell, Jane Kimberly, Carol Marshall, Nancy Leverett, Joanne Robinson, Donna Dunlap, Carolyn Tramill, LaDonna Subert, Roxie Rendina, Pat Bailey, Beverly Davis

Footman: James Tyler

Outriders: Andy Schaffer Jr., George Calvert, Loran Gum, Forrest Gainer

Episode I

INTRODUCTION

Osage Indians: Bill Hennessy, Jr., Tom Sharper, Oneida Berg, Bess Bowers, Mary McKinstry, Freda Rau, Carmelita Weathers, Ora Jean Carr, Louis Chilcoat, Nancy Chilcoat, Louella Chilcoat, Larry McDonough, Ronald Briece, Myrna Brewer

Covered Wagon Family: Mrs. Eldon Budd, Diana Budd, Geoffrey Budd

Episode II

"THE FRENCH"

Scene 1—"Etienne Veniard de Bourgmont views the Bend of the Missouri"

De Bourgmont: Cole Wells

Soldiers: Roger Coffey, Ross Peeler

Scene 2—"The Court of Louis XV—France"

King: Frank Stein

Queen: Virginia Green

Ladies in Waiting: Virginia Winters, Betty Skinner, Marian King, Delores Smith, Marcia Mitchum, Dalene Smith

Ladies of the Court: Cherrie Green, Dolores Crow, Rita Snilling, Betty Newton, Carol Berry, Peggy Rose, Peggy Cock, Anabele Jackson, Pat Linderman, Jo Ann Tricarico, Rita Postlewait, Norma Martin, Janice Coffman, Janett Drury, Laura Beth McDaniel, Sadi Stearns, Mary Jo Evans
(Participants courtesy of Dorothy Lee, Inc.)

Men of the Court: Bob Lettas, John Hayter, Eddie Bryant, Rodney Horton, Wendy Boswill, Bob Sommer, Kern Burton, Jerry Burton, Richard Bower, Tom Zang, George Gutkneck, Bob Richmond, Edward Callon, H. F. Green, Bob Gee, Bill Herberger

Palace Guards: Otto Berg, Carl Lamb, Clifford Bryant, Ernie Shoemaker, Wayne Hurlbut, James Tyler, Brad Randall, Russell Steen

Lackeys: Archie Villines, Sidney Spiller, Bob Huff, Oscar Winslow

Princess of the Missouri: "Boots" Hurst

Indian Chieftains: Head Chieftain—Sam Cipriana. J. Eddie Owen, Bill Laughlin, Tommy J. Vincent, F. Forrest Shane, Warren Lee Messinger, Bill Standing, B. Jack Neas, Kenneth Wood, Jerry A. Smith, John Rabuse

Episode III

"THE COMING OF THE AMERICANS"

Scene 1—"The First American—Daniel Morgan Boone"

Daniel Boone: Thayer Townsend

Scene 2—"Transfer of the Upper Louisiana Purchase"

French Officers: Paul Kapp, Bob Harris

Sergeant: Clifford Adams

French Soldiers:

U.S.A. Officers: Wayne Harris, Frank Bowers

U.S.A. Sergeant:

U.S.A. Soldiers: Barney Green, David Phillips, Tom Hollcroft

Scene 3—"The Treaty of Fort Osage"

U.S.A. Officers: (Same as Scene 2)

Soldiers:

Pierre Chouteau: Sam Bergner

Indian Chiefs: Bill Hennessey, Jr., Tom Sharper, Art Drayer, Larry McDonough, Ronald Briece

Scene 4—"Major Stephen H. Long's—Great Western Engineer"

Indian Chiefs: (Same as Scene 3)

Indian Braves: Frank Bowers, Jr., Dale Philpott, Bob Hodges, Chuck Barthol, Robert Wilcox, Freddie Cole, Donald Lehman, Jimmy Flynn, Larry Thomas

Indian Squaws: Lucille Ballard, Louise Ballard, Myrna Brewer, Mary Weddendorf, Carmelita Weathers, Mrs. Willie Edwards, Bess Bowers, Marjorie Ungor, Audray Stainbrook, Betty Frederick, Mary McKinstry, Mary Ann McKinstry, Freda Rau, Oneita Berg, Ora Jean Carr

Indian Children: Beverly Sweeney, Nancy McKinstrey, Margaret McKinstry, Marilyn Williams, Nancy Chilcoat, Louella Chilcoat, Louis Chilcoat, Earl Carson, Tyrone Carson

Major Long: Wayne Harris

U.S.A. Soldiers and Officers: Personnel Same as Scene 2

Episode IV

"FOUNDING OF THE COMMUNITY OF KANSAS"

Scene 1—"French Folk Dancers"

Delores Munguia, Arlene Donovan, Charlotte Knox, Joan Hurlbut, Virginia Richman, Sherry Dee Tipton, Marguarite Noble, Nancy Faureau, Marilyn Brett, Thelma Jarvis, Fern Nelson, Janice Austin, Jo Ann Lipps, Pat Park, Betty Brotemarkle

Sandra Stockamp, Beverly Childers, Dalene Smith, Marcia Mitchum, Peggy Rose
(Courtesy of Dorothy Lee, Inc.)

Pioneer Men: Don Dally, Arnold Hydeman, Tom Newby, Harvy Wisdom, Frank Kozak, Frank Dally, Clarence Neil, Elmer Sundquist, Joseph Carolan, George Burroughs, Frank Hugelman, George Calvert, Loran Gum, Andy Schaffer, Jr., Don Schwartz, Jim Burke, James Arthur, Leonard Merl, Ken Hardin, John Holman, Wayne Harris, Roy Newman, Stanley Bernhardt, Virgil R. Leslie, Francis Carter, Lawrence Jones, Frank Thomas, Larry Thomas, Carl Thomas, Jack Kitchin, Lewis Clayton, Michael Franke

Pioneer Women: Grace Newby, Mary Schweiger, Margaret Kleinman, Mary Oshimo, Mrs. Eldon Budd, Mrs. Harvey Wisdom, Mrs. J. F. Carolan, Mrs. James Hide, Mrs. Albert F. Hinshaw, Mrs. F. C. Dally, Mrs. F. J. Kozak, Mrs. E. R. Sundquist, Mrs. Arnold Hydeman, Mrs. Walter Hillis, Mrs. Clarence Neil, Helen Meiners, Ruth Calvert, La Von Rambo, Madge P. William, Mrs. Charles Burroughs, Amy Hardin, Audrey Merl, Mildred Wellington, Ella May Newman, Lola Marrott, Mrs. L. W. Simcoe, Lucinda Finley, Helen Gilwee, Elizabeth Shannon, Marie Leamon, Pat Brown, Wilda Sweeney, Mrs. Lewis Clayton, Mrs. Earl Carson, Mrs. Ed Leonard, Mrs. Frank Thomas, Mrs. Carl Thomas

Pioneer Girls: Elaine Hydeman, Valinda Sundquist, Grace Wisdom, Judith Ann Henshaw, Betsy Carolan, Sharon Hide, Diana Budd, Rosemary Franke, Donna Kozak, Sandra Kozak, Patty Williams, Lynne Merl, Sheryle Calvert, Judy Carter

Pioneer Boys: Geoffrey Budd, Jimmy Hide, Louis Franke, Don Franke, Francis Franke, Lloyd Franke, Eugene Franke, Terry Dally, Mike Merl, Dean Marriot, Dennis Neil, Kent Simcoe, Terry Simcoe

French Folk Dancers: Dolores Munquia, Joan Hurlbut, Virginia

Richman, Sherry Dee Tipton, Margarite Noble, Jo Ann Lipps, Pat Park, Nancy Favreau, Marilyn Brett, Thelma Jarvis, Beverly Childers, Dalene Smith, Marcia Mitchum, Carol Berry, Peggy Rose, Cherrie Green, Joan Tricarico, Sandra Partridge (Courtesy of Dorothy Lee, Inc.)

Scene 2—"Auction Sale of Kansas Town Lots"
Squire Tate: Wesley Rambo
Pioneers: Jim Burke, James Arthur, George Calvert, Loran Gum, George Burroughs, E. R. Sundquist, Frank Hugelman, A. H. Hydeman, Andy Schaffer, Jr., Joseph Carolan, Harvey Wisdom, Don Schwartz

Scene 3—"The Indians Moved West"
Personnel same as Episode III—Scene 4

Scene 4—"Benton Prophecy"
Senator Thomas Hart Benton: Eldon Budd
Men: Leonard Merl, Walter Hillis, J. B. Hulbert, Bill Williams, Wayne Harris, Ken Sweeney
Women: Mrs. Charlie Burroughs, Mrs. Walter Hillis, Mrs. Elmer Sundquist, Amy Hardin

Episode V

"WESTPORT — 1833 - 1853"

Scene 1—"An Early Street Scene in Westport"
Pioneer Personnel same as previous scenes
John C. McCoy: Bill Williams
Francis Parkman: Ken Sweeney
Jim Bridger: Robert Cummings
Kit Carson: Robert Renau
Col. Doniphan: J. B. Hulbert
Mexican Dancers: Rosie Hurtado, Alice Bernal, Refugia Hernandez, Esther Gutieretz, Clementine Hurtado, Lupe Aquirre
Duenna: Marie Arredondo
Mexican Cabelleros:
Soldiers: Chester F. Smith, E. C. Melstrom, Forrest Gainer, Tom Hollcroft, Barney Green, David Phillips, Marvin Tracy

Scene 2—"The California Gold Rush"
Personnel same as Episode IV—Scene 1
Mary: Wilda Sweeney
Sam: Ken Sweeney
Leader: Leonard Merl
Padre: M. S. Hensley
Sick Man: Clarence Neil
Wife: Mrs. Clarence Neil
Son: Dennis Neil
Daughter:

Scene 3—"A Showboat Highlight"
Heroine: Agnes Kass
Hero: Phil Schwab
Villian: James Tyler
Mother: Dorothy Baker
Barker: Jimmy Brown
Quartette:

Episode VI

"GROWTH & WAR"

Scene 1—"Kansas City—Slavery Proponents and Abolitionists"
Civilian Men: Roy Miller, Alex Boris, William Rister, Oliver Shephard, Sherman Holmes, Carl Lamb, Jay Lamb, Henry Nelson, Larry Zirkle, Jim Newby, W. L. Wilson, Charles Edwards, Ross Goodman, James Crockett, Cleo Sutton, Virgil Lewellen, Leslie Smith, Harry Lovelace, James Woodmansee, Sandy Lewis, Everett Burgett, Paul Rickard, Bob Schooling, Raymond Heidman, Herbert Handslip, Jack Peacock, Robert Hanson, Fontelle Mahen, Jay Finney, Hugo Haselhorst, A. C. Taylor, Vernon Sherrill, Bill Fullen, Barney Rinard, Charles Young, Harry Crabb
Civilian Women: Lillian Debus, Armedia Sutton, Elfa Bisbee, Effie Mae Smith, Iva Lovelace, Carol Astry, Reba Woodmansee, Naomi Richey, Clara Lewis, Josephine Lett, Giniva Hanslip, Adelia Davis, Pat Brown, Pauline Waddell, Mary Zumwalt, Dorothy Jacobson, Leta Miller, Vera Nagourney, Zella Rickard, Helen Lane, Goldie Sanders, Shirley Arnold, Sylvia Boris, Alice Miller, Helen Rister, Dorothy Shephard, Velma Sherrill, Joan Degenhardt, Lorene Lamb, Bonnie Bisbee, Jackie Hanson, Ethel Johnson, Wanda Cook, Minabel Jergins, Bertha Jones, Anabel Klos, Helen Finney, Marjorie Haselhorst, Lucille Taylor, Margaret Burgett, Mary Lee Bagby, Selma Holmes
Girls: Kay Lamb, Denise Sherrill, Sharon Smith, Romona Klos, Barbara Burgett, Sandra Finney

Boys: Gordon Smith, Terry Klos, Leonard Taylor, Skipper Burgett, George Burgett, John Jergins

Scene 2—"The Civil War"
Telegrapher:
Major Van Horn:
Officers: Wm. Young
Messenger:
Old Man:
Boy:

Scene 3—"The Battle of Westport"
Personnel same as Episode VI—Scene 1
General Curtis: Wm. Young
Officer:
Soldiers: Loren Debus, Robert Harrod, P. V. Sherrill, Glen Bisbee, Clifford Adams, Robert Miller, Ralph Lane, Tim Gonzales, Ray Morrison, William Young, John Spear, Jerry Finney, Ward McDonald, David Swyer, Robert Snyder, Jim Williams

Episode VII

"RAILROADS AND CATTLE"

Scene 1—"Opening of the Hannibal Bridge"
Railroad Engineer: Ben Brooks
Octave Chanute:
Kersey Coates:
Congressman Van Horn:
Mayor F. R. Long:
Charles Kearney:
Townfolk—Same as Episode VI—Scene 1

Scene 2—"The Cattle Industry"
Dancers: Cowgirls: Harriet Jamieson, Joanne Wait, Evelyn Shabason, Charlene Williams, Barbara Clemons, Joan McFadden, Shirley Stinson, Donna Simmons, Ethelyn Upp, Diane Petterson. Cowboys: J. Eddie Owen, Bill Laughlin, Tommy J. Vincent, F. Forrest Shane, Warren Lee Messinger, Bill Standing, B. Jack Neas, Kenneth Wood, Jerry A. Smith, John Rabuse
Guitar Soloist:

Episode VIII

"THE SEVENTIES AND EIGHTIES"

Scene 1—"The Office of Marshal Tom Speers"
Tom Speers: John Holman
Wyatt Earp: Stanley Bernhardt
"Wild Bill" Hickok: Andy Schaffer, Jr.
Jack Gallagher: Forrest Gainer
Billy Dixon: Loran Gum
Jim Hanrahan: Jim Burke
Tom O'Keefe: George Calvert
Kirk Jordan: James Arthur

Scene 2—"Jesse James Robs the Industrial Exposition Box Office"
Cashier: Ralph McClenahan
Jessie James: Earl Myers
Frank James: Vernon Engelhaupt
Younger Brothers: Milton Fletcher, Tom Devine
Posse: Personnel same as Scene 1

Scene 3—"President and Mrs. Grover Cleveland"
President Cleveland: Brad Randall
Mrs. Cleveland: Jean Humphreys
Officials: Carl Lamb, Sherwood Parsons, George Stark, R. H. Denson
Wives: Lorene Lamb, Louise Lawson

Episode IX

"THE GAY NINETIES"

Scene 1—"A Picture of the Gay 90's
Mayor: Sam Bergner
Life Guards: Jay Lamb, Tom Devine
Constables: Oscar Winslow, Sidney Spiller, David Watson
Medicine Doctor: Jimmie Brown
Mailman: Phil Schwab
Vendor: Russel Steen
Bathing Beauties: Mary Evalyn, Marbeth Hopman, Martha Anderson, Connie Jones, Mona Halliburton, Evalyn Eyer, Nieta Fromuth, Phyllis Graf, Betty Storm
Can Can Dancers: Evelyn Hedden, Barbara Hartley, Maryetta Johnson, Louis Garrett, Gay McGuire, Freddie Pound, Gyenn Shay, Charlotte Manson, Grace Nubelo, Jean Ravenscroft,

Delores Klenke, Betty Bende
Men: James Tyler, Sherwood Parsons, Clifford Bryant, S. W. McGinnis, Otto Berg, George Stark, Wayne Hurlbut, Carl Lamb, Jay Lamb, Archie Villines, Keith Ludden, Robert Huff, James Wright, Bill Wade, Bob Huff, Don Quisenberry, E. C. Melstrom
Women: Doris Griffith, Nanette Dennis, Barbara MacIntosh, Mary Jean Horney, Georgia Tyler, Mary Lewellyn, Carolyn Ford, Eleanor Hurlbut, Lucille Tyler, Ida Nelson, Jean Faith, Deryl Jones, Ruth Wing, Amy Young, Mathilde Brosseau, Joanne Vaughn, Mary Jo Lanergan, Mary Ann Costello, Peggy Arensberg, Bobbie Stolor, Julia Fortner, Edna Jones, Marjorie Alleman, Edna Davidson, Marlyn Parsons, Mrs. Charles Anderson, Mrs. Keith Ludden, Shirley Look, Iris Bernstine, Linda Levy, Ann Huff, Helen Mueller, Zula Randall, Marbeth Hopmann, Dorothy Quisenberry
Boys: Gary Lewllyn, Gerry Gunter, Clifford Senzee
Girls: Marlene Stolor, Kay Lamb, Jacklyn Alexander, Norma Kay Senzee, Linda Parsons

Scene 2—"Convention Hall Burns"

Fire Chief: Wayne Hurlburt

Episode X

"THE TWENTIETH CENTURY"

Scene 1—"The American Royal Live Stock and Horse Show"
Personnel same as in Episode IX

Scene 2—"The First Automobile Show"
All personnel from Episode IX—Scene 1

Scene 3—"World War I"
Personnel from Episode IX—Scene 1

Scene 4—"Dedication of the Liberty Memorial"
General Baron Jacques: Tom Devine
General Armando Diaz: Ralph McClenahan
Vice-President Calvin Coolidge: Joseph Carolan
Marshall Foch: Tom Newby
David Lord Beatty: Milton Fletcher
Gen. John J. Pershing: Riley Reeves

Episode XI

"A FAMOUS KANSAS CITY MEMORY —

Scene 1—"Epperson's Minstrels"
Girl Dancers: Harriet Jamieson, Joanne Wait, Evelyn Shabason, Charlene Williams, Barbara Clemons, Joan McFadden, Shirley Stinson, Donna Simmons, Ethelyn Upp, Diane Patterson
Boy Dancers: J. Eddie Owen, Sam Cipriana, Bill Laughlin, Tommy J. Vincent, F. Forrest Shane, Warren Lee Messinger, Bill Standing, B. Jack Neas, Kenneth Wood, Jerry A. Smith, John Rabuse

Episode XII

"TRUMAN AND WAR"

Scene 1—"The News of Pearl Harbor"
Two Kansas City Homes:
First Family: Father: Wesley Rambo, Mother: LaVon Rambo, Boys: Bob Harris, Paul Kapp, Girl: Judy Carter
Second Family: Father: Sidney Spiller, Mother: Mrs. Willie Edwards, Boy: Delmas Montgomery, Girls: Carmelita Weathers, Carlotta Hoard

Scene 2—"The Declaration of War"
Scene 3—"Kansas City Girds for War"
Army, Navy, Marine, Merchant Marine, WACS, WAVES, WAFS, SPARS, Army Nurses, Navy Nurses, Red Cross, Salvation Army, Civilian Defense, Gray Ladies, Women's Motor Corps, Labor

Scene 4—"The Presidential Election"
Scene 5—"The Death of the President"
Personnel same as Scene 1

Scene 6—"The War is Ended"
Personnel same as previous scene

Finale

United Nations: Jane Rabb, Ethel Parry, Mary Brislin, Louise Buffington, Helen Hainje, Virginia McCarthy, Margaret White, Betty Lou Miller, Helen Lohmeyer, Jane Shoemaker, Vivien Pecoraro, Nyla Tipton, Lee Tipton, Marie Yoders, Vivian Wolf, Marian Thudium, Frances Landsiedel, Mildred Barnett, Betty Davidson, Mildred Reniker, Geneva Duncan, Dorothy Stratemeier, Elnor Stratemeier, Lorene Cave, Jane McDonald, Virginia Olsen, Doris Ryan, Rose Marie Purdam, Doris Early, Ruby Mindrup, Ann Sniezek, Dorothy Gleeson, Eleanor Orr, Elizabeth Dykes, Billie Stillman, Shirley Jones, Mary Stockman, Margaret Minton, Kay Bradshaw, Jean Powers, Mary Jo Matthews, Marnie Silcock, Thelma Mix, Emma Kyle, Lydia Brooks, Frankye Cameron, Donna Lewis, Rosemary Piper, Mary Ann Hanlin, Helen Martin, Nancy McDonald, Grace Misner
(Participants Courtesy of Beta Sigma Phi Sorority)
United Nations Flag Bearers: Dorothea Squires, Margaret Lewis, Virginia Joe Sipes, Eva Bailey, Margaret Aimes, Billie Crawford, Betty Thornsherry, Mary Schmidt, Elaine Storks, Ferne Estep, Martha Baese, Dorothy Sullivan, Mary O'Brien, Carolyn Flanagan, Ann Davison, Frances Wolfkill, June Hale, Audry Smith, Eleanor Peabody, Orpha Cecil, Helen Mulligan, Dorothy Morrone, Ruth DeFries, Shirley Blickhan, Josephine Hamner, Neva Mathes, Marjorie Gallemore, Delores McMaster, Billy Hungerford, Beverly Thompson, Gladys Kinder, Majorie Weiner, Ruth Danforth, Joan Hutcheson, Mary Margaret Ring, Dorothy Kemper, Doris Kemper, Patty Mattimore, Delores Worth, Audrey Walmer, Orlette Latterer, Nioma Brooks, Eleanor Mundis, Nancy Wilder, Betty Gibbs, Maxine Keitel, Ann Feris, Ila Mae Kampschroeder
(Participants Courtesy of the Beta Sigma Sorority)
United States Ladies: Same as Prologue
U. S. A. Flag Bearers: Same as Prologue

"KANSAS CITY FACES ITS SECOND CENTURY"

Narrators: James Burke, Robert Kennedy, Harvey Brunswick, Art Ellison, Janet Ewing
Alternates: Doreen Kuhl, Jack Layton

CENTENNIAL CHORUS

Eugene Christy, Conductor
Hugh Sandidge, Associate Conductor
Clerence Farrar, Associate Conductor
Betty Jean Warrel, Linda Coleman, John R. Guemple, Joan Crain, Ernest Pendleton, Dorothy Brunn, Ann Crawford, Jim Peterson, Theols (Teddy) Walchter, Antoinette Budd, Sandra Stule, Stephen A. Raphel, Mary Lou White, Phil Cline, Harry Sherrill, Shirley Goss, Alice Mae Turpin, Noble Kergerreis, Virginia Stocker, Sally Barts, Romona Abbott, Nancy Shelton, Neil Walhen, Jim Scalisi, Joette Pecoraro, Chet Laveles, Jackie Morris, Dorothy Fry, Norma J. Hawk, Barbara Hazelbacker, Maurice Greeley, William Ross Perry, David Whitington, Robin Sperry, Jean Lewis, Patty McDaniel, Paul Frazer, Diane Valentine, Nadine Conrad, Anne Mandracchia, Louis Potts, Tom Moran, Judith Penrase, June Williams, Cora Anne Smith, Shirley Ann Vehlewald, Nancy Moore, Meta Ann Kuechl, Ruth Ann Hall, Grace Mack, Shirley Stinson, Bonnie Wood, Joan Siler, Nona Atheisson, Dorothy Linnerson, Janet Sanders, Doris McNish, Grace J. Frisby, Louise Frisby, Donna Hargis, Shirley Richardson, Nancy Neighbors, Carol Roseen, Barbara Long, Mary Flener, Janice Robinson, Jean Wahlstrom, C. L. Wade, Celia Toney, Barbara Rosier, Duveen Kaser, Beverly Rosier, Shirley Landis, Dorothy Oliver, Ruth Robinson, Betty Harper, Forestina Rogers, Barbara Ade, Lola Donigan, Esther Laughlin, Darline Long, Marion Meyer, Don McRoberts, Robert E. Blackwell, Jerry Dunn, Joan Freeman, Jeanerre Francis, Jim Duffin, Leta Wade, Fred Featherstone, Mary Welsh, Loretta Waddell, Bernetta Duncan, Jane C. Shane, Sally Moore, Evelyn Hodden, Elaine Gatrost, R. E. Meeink, Irene Bell, Maude Rice, Merl Reed, Calvin J. Reed, Marellen McDouthat, Mildred M. Kelly, Rose Aguirre, Josephine Aguirre, Nancy Myers, Eleanore Peacock, Mrs. Mary Dye, Beverly Mittie, Mrs. C. C. Ehlers, Ruth Higginbotham, Lois Crecther, Pat Bryan, Vella Bryan, Lillian Shelton,
Mrs. E. G. Carlson, Dr. E. G. Carlson, Elsie Figzgerald, Freda Henson, Tom Roach, Nancy Stebbins, Ruby Scott, Ruth MacLachlan, Nancy Bell, Winifred Anderson, A. T. Morgan, Mrs. Berkey, Mrs. Marilyn Ehlers, Miss Elizabeth Bennett, Mrs. Ruth Johnson, Elizabeth Boles, Lloyd Boles, Ted Budd, Barbara J. Black, Beverly Moen, Loraler Doell, Anna Marie Hessler, Linnea Peterson, Lora Porter, Mary Robinson, Toni Lasta, Bette Melluish, Marion Shelton, Carol Hartig, Gerald Chriss, Fred Eichpok, Josephine Trabon, Winnifred Campbell, Peggy Marts, Emma Shirley, Marie C. Brown, Bernadine Fowler, Oda Sandidge, Mildred Carlson, Chloe Simpson, Fredie Marz, Francis Oglevie, Dorothy Gumminger, Margaret L. Snyder, Paul Edward, V. McCue, Harry Owen Ogg, Betty Jean Lichtenberger, R. M. Lichtenberger, Rachel Rue, Janis Hightower, Darlene Zweissler, Katherine Edi, Duane L. Coltharp, Clastine Cooper, Maxine H. Perine, Margaret Farren, Sylvia Stephens, Betty Graham, May Dorth.

★ BIBLIOGRAPHY ★

BOOKS:

Bergreen, Laurence. *As Thousands Cheer.* New York: Penguin Books. 1990.

Bordman, Gerald. *American Musical Comedy.* New York: Oxford University Press. 1982.

Bordman, Gerald. *American Musical Revue.* New York: Oxford University Press. 1985.

Brown, Theodore A. & Lyle W. Dorsett. *K.C. A History of Kansas City, Missouri.* Boulder, Colorado: Pruett Publishing Company. 1978.

Engel, Lehman. *The American Musical Theatre.* New York: The Macmillan Company. 1967.

Ewen, David. *The Story of America's Musical Theatre.* Philadelphia & New York: Chilton Company. 1961.

Green, Stanley. *The World of Musical Comedy.* New York: Da Capo Press, Inc. 1980.

Hallmark Edition Staff. *Kansas City.* Kansas City, Missouri: Hallmark Cards, Inc. 1973.

Hibbert, Christopher. *Gilbert & Sullivan.* New York: American Heritage Publishing Co., Inc. 1976.

Historical Kansas City Foundation. *Kansas City, Missouri An Architectural History 1826-1976.* Kansas City, Missouri: The Lowell Press. 1979.

Kislan, Richard. *The Musical.* Englewood Cliffs, New Jersey: Prentice-Hall, Inc. 1980.

Lerner, Alan Jay. *The Street Where I Live.* New York: W. W. Norton & Co. 1978.

Lox, Roger & Frederick Smith. *The Great Song Thesaurus.* New York: Oxford University Press. 1984.

Mattfeld, Jules. *Variety Music Cavalcade.* Englewood Cliffs, New Jersey: Prentice Hall, Inc. 1971.

Neufeldt, Victoria and David B. Guralnik, editors. *Webster's New World Dictionary.* (New York: 1988).

Sampson, Henry T. *Blacks in Blackface.* New Jersey & London: The Scarecrow Press Inc. 1980.

Sandy, Wilda. *Here Lies Kansas City.* Kansas City, Missouri: Bennett Schneider Publishing. 1984.

Smith, Cecil & Glenn Litton. *Musical Comedy in America.* New York: Theatre Arts Books. 1981.

Traubner, Richard. *Operetta- A Theatrical History.* Garden City, New York: Doubleday & Company, Inc. 1983.

NEWSPAPERS:

Clip File — indicates that information is part of the Kansas City, Missouri Main Library's clip file on Starlight Theatre.

"About...G. Philippe de Rosier." Starlight Theatre souvenir program, August 15-21 1960. p. 15.

"About...Mrs. Virginia Donovan." Starlight Theatre souvenir program, August 15-21 1960. p. 25.

"About...The Costumes." Starlight Theatre souvenir program, July 31-August 6 1961.

"A Fine Starlight Year." *The Kansas City Star,* 7 September 1952.

"All Would Sit Near Queen." *The Kansas City Star*, 11 November 1926.

"The 'Americana' Composer." Starlight Theatre souvenir program, July 14-20 1958. p. 10.

"A Salute to Civic Progress." Starlight Theatre souvenir program, July 27-August 2 1953.

" A Salute to Civic Progress." Starlight Theatre souvenir program, July 18-24 1955.

"A Second Stage." Starlight Theatre souvenir program, June 9-15 1958. p. 24.

"A Starlight Bid Date." *The Kansas City Star*, 15 March 1954.

"A Thrills Mark." *The Kansas City Times*, 5 July 1950.

"Backstage at Starlight—Carpentry." Starlight Theatre souvenir program, June 27-July 3 1977. p. 24.

"Backstage at Starlight: Sound." Starlight Theatre souvenir program, July 18-24 1977. p. 30.

"Backstage in Wardrobe." Starlight Theatre souvenir program, July 25-31 1977. p. 22.

"Behind a Starlight Scene Stands a Master Carpenter." *The Kansas City Star*, 22 June 1952. p. 11C.

"The Best At Starlight." *The Kansas City Star,* 10 February 1954.

"Biggest Year At Starlight." *The Kansas City Star,* 7 September 1953.

"Bill Symon's Civic Success." *The Kansas City Times,* 26 January 1966.

Bylaws of Starlight Theatre Association of Kansas City, Inc. 23 October 1980.

"Choreography by...Harding Dorn." Starlight Theatre souvenir program, July 11-17 1966.

"City's Life in Pageantry." *The Kansas City Star*, 4 June 1950. p. 1.

Clark, Champ. "Kansas City's History Lives Anew in Spectacle of Vivid Scenes." *The Kansas City Star*, 28 May 1950.

"D. Aldon Ferrara." Starlight Theatre souvenir program, August 20-26 1973.

Diagram of Seating Chart and Ticket Prices, Starlight Theatre business office, summer 1989.

Doohan, John. "Starlight Theatre Can Trace Birth to 1926 Visit of Queen of Romania." *The Kansas City Times,* 18 June 1952. p. 50.

Dvorak, John. "Starlight Begs, Borrows Props for Authenticity." *The Kansas City Times,* 3 August 1971.

Dvorak, John. "Starlight Loss $48,000." *The Kansas City Times*, 3 October 1975. p. 3A.

Fisher, Brenda. "Artist Behind the Scenery." *The Kansas City Times*, 15 June 1972. Clip file.

Fitzpatrick, James C. "Curtain Ready to Rise on a New Starlight." *The Kansas City Times,* 21 May 1981. p. B-2.

"Form a Student Board." *The Kansas City Star,* 14 June 1956.

"Form a Theatre Group." *The Kansas City Star*, 15 May 1956.

Foster, William. "Starlight: Relaxed and Ready." *The Independence Examiner,* 19 June 1961. p. 10.

Fowler, Richard B. "Leaders in Our Town." *The Kansas City Star*, 2 December 1951. p. E1

Funk, Jerry. "Backstage Starlight Theatre." *Independence Pictorial News,* 12 July 1962. p. 1.

Funk, Jerry. "Backstage Starlight Theatre." *Independence Pictorial News,* 2 August 1962. p. 1.

Funk, Jerry. "Backstage Starlight Theatre." *Independence Pictorial News,* 9 August 1962. p. 1.

Funk, Jerry. Kansas City, Missouri. Letter, 1 July 1990. Kathleen Thorne, Eugene, Oregon.

Gardner, James N. "One Man Job in Starlight Direction and Choreography." *The Kansas City Times,* 17 June 1971. Clip file.

"Genius....at Scenery and Lighting." Starlight Theatre souvenir program, July 3-9 1961.

Halsey, Randy. Independence, Missouri. Letter, 26 February 1990. Kathleen Thorne, Eugene, Oregon.

Hartmann, Alice. "Impresario Took 'Practical Side.'" *The Kansas City Times,* 15 May 1975.

Haskell, Henry C. "Scanning the Arts." *The Kansas City Star,* 28 June 1964. Clip file.

Haskins, John. "Whatever Happened to Starlight Theatre." *The Kansas City Star,* 7 September 1975. p. 7E.

Kansas City Missouri Parks Board Annual Report. 1941.

Kaye, Joseph. "Long Span by Costume Company." *The Kansas City Star,* 23 August 1967. Clip file.

Knickerbocker, Laura. "Starlight Past Recalled." *The Kansas City Times,* 1 August 1974.

Laird, Landon. "About Town." *The Kansas City Times,* 28 January 1966.

Laird, Landon. "Gay Porter Revue." *The Kansas City Times,* 2 August 1955. Clip file.

"Lead With 'Peter Pan.'" *The Kansas City Star,* 4 March 1956.

"Maestro Fiore...Composer." Starlight Theatre souvenir program, July 14-20 1958.

McQueeny, Jim. "Starlight Preview and Review." Starlight Theatre souvenir program, June 23-29 1952. p. 33.

McQueeny, Jim. "The Starlight Story." Starlight Theatre souvenir program, July 30-August 5 1951.

McQueeny, Jim. "The Story Behind 10 Years of Starlight Theatre." Starlight Theatre souvenir program, June 27-July 3 1960. p. 18.

McQueeny, Jim. "The Story Behind 10 Years of Starlight Theatre." Starlight Theatre souvenir program, July 4-17 1960.

McQueeny, Jim. "The Story Behind 10 Years of Starlight Theatre." Starlight Theatre souvenir program, August 1-7 1961.

"Meet Mrs. Hydeman." Starlight Theatre souvenir program, August 4-10 1975.

Morgan, Sally. "She Dolls Up 'Dolly.'" *The Kansas City Star,* 30 June 1970. p. 10.

"Needs $150,000 for Starlight." *The Kansas City Times,* 11 February 1970.

"OK On Show Shelter." *The Kansas City Star,* 12 January 1954.

"OK Starlight Plans." *The Kansas City Times,* 11 February 1954.

"On With Theatre Work." *The Kansas City Star,* 9 March 1953.

"One Hit Show After Another...All Summer Long." Starlight Theatre souvenir program, June 19-25 1961.

Parker, Maurica Campbell. "Speaking the Public Mind." *The Kansas City Times,* 18 September 1975.

Picture Caption. *The Kansas City Times,* 17 March 1954.

Picture Caption. *The Kansas City Star,* 27 February 1963.

"Queen Here Tonight." *The Kansas City Star,* 11 November 1926.

Rose, Stan. "What's the Matter with Starlight?" *The Johnson County Sun,* 6 August 1975. p. 2A.

Satchell, Michael J. "Rock and Brass Resound Under Starlit Sky." *The Kansas City Times,* 23 June 1970. Clip file.

"Seek Starlight With No Deficit." *The Kansas City Times,* 10 September 1958.

"Shelter at the Starlight." *The Kansas City Times,* 12 September 1953.

"Show Shelter An Aim." *The Kansas City Star,* 3 January 1954.

Skylines—Kansas City Chapter of the American Institute of Architects, September 1956, Vol. 6 Number 9.

"Starlight: It's a Kansas City Tradition." Starlight Theatre souvenir program, June 20-26 1983. p. 27.

"Starlight Looks to Change." *The Kansas City Times,* 28 January 1966.

Starlight Theatre Association Report on All Shows Held 1951-1979, 4 February 1980.

"Stories Backstage." Starlight Theatre souvenir program, July 13-19 1964. p. 29.

"Theatre League is Back for This Season." Starlight Theatre souvenir program, July 25-31 1983. p. 7.

"34,200 Costumes Later." Starlight Theatre souvenir program, July 31-August 6 1961. p. 17.

"Who's Who...in the Cast." Starlight Theatre souvenir program, July 4-17 1960.

"Wild Oxen on Stage." *The Kansas City Times,* 7 June 1950.

"William M. Symon's Promotion." *The Kansas City Journal Post,* 10 September 1932. p. 11.

"The World Premiere." Starlight Theatre souvenir program, July 14-20, 1958. p. 4.

INTERVIEWS:

Adelman, Dr. Arthur. Lifelong friend of Tony Ferrara, former general manager at Starlight Theatre. Interview by author. 13 March 1990. Prairie Village, Kansas.

Allen, Vicki. Former dance ensemble member at Starlight Theatre. Interview by author. 9 April 1990. Overland Park, Kansas.

Allison, Jack. Director at Starlight Theatre. Interview by author. 25 March 1990. New York City, New York.

Armijo, Lilian (Mrs. Jerry Funk). Former ensemble singer at Starlight Theatre. Interview by author. 13 July 1989. Kansas City, Missouri.

Bartosh, Kathy. Former dance ensemble member at Starlight Theatre. Interview by author. 9 April 1990. Overland Park, Kansas.

Berger, Richard. Former producing director of Starlight Theatre. Interview by author. 19 November, 1989. Los Angeles, California.

Bookman, Kirk. Lighting designer for Starlight Theatre. Interview by author. 25 March 1990. New York City, New York.

Charone, Irwin. Second most frequently seen male performer at Starlight Theatre. Interview by author. 6 July 1990. Kansas City, Missouri.

Childers, Harold. Former electrician at Starlight Theatre. Interview by author. 31 March 1990. Shawnee Mission, Kansas.

Coulter, Dorothy (Mrs. Joseph Hall). Most frequently seen leading lady at Starlight Theatre. Interview by author. 19 April and 2 May 1990. Leawood, Kansas.

Culver, Edwin III. Chief executive officer and general manager for the St. Louis Municipal Opera. Interview by author. 28 June 1990. St. Louis, Missouri.

Dean, William. Set painter for Starlight Theatre. Interview by author. 1 July 1989. Kansas City, Missouri.

De Rosier, G. Philippe. Former resident set designer for Starlight Theatre. Interview by author. 6 November 1989 and 18 January 1990. Santa Fe, New Mexico.

Dokoudovoska, Tatiana. Former featured dancer at Starlight and former instructor at the Kansas City Conservatory of Dance. Interview by author. 12 July, 1990. Kansas City, Missouri.

Doohan, John. Former box office manager for Starlight Theatre and former newspaper reporter for *The Kansas City Star* and *The Kansas City Times*. Interview by author. 11 July 1989. Kansas City, Missouri.

Doohan, Mary. Former employee in the publicity office at Starlight Theatre. Interview by author. 11 July 1989. Kansas City, Missouri.

Ferrara, Aldon. Son of the former manager of Starlight Theatre and himself the former production manager at Starlight Theatre. Interview by author. 17 July 1989 and 27 January 1990. Kansas City, Missouri.

Ferrara, Mark. Son of the former manager of Starlight Theatre and himself the former director of publicity for Starlight Theatre. Interview by author. 31 March 1990. Kansas City, Missouri.

Fiore, Roland. Former musical director at Starlight Theatre. Interview by author. 4 June 1990. New Hope, Pennsylvania.

Flynn, Monica Doohan. Executive director of the Wichita Children's Theatre. Interview by author. 18 July 1990. Wichita, Kansas.

Franano, Frank. Music contractor for the Starlight Theatre. Interview by author. 10 March 1990. Kansas City, Missouri.

Funk, Jerry. Former stage manager for Starlight Theatre. Interview by author. 13 July and 12 December 1989 and 28 March 1990. Kansas City, Missouri.

Hall, Joseph. Long-time friend of Richard Berger. Interview by author. 19 April 1990 and 2 May 1990 and 2 April 1992. Leawood, Kansas.

Halsey, Randy. Master carpenter and technical director at Starlight Theatre. Interview by author. 17 July 1989 and 30 January 1990 and 12 March 1990. Kansas City, Missouri.

Hogan, John. Former stagehand at Starlight Theatre. Interview by author. 19 July 1990. Kansas City, Missouri.

Krikorian, Al. Former property master for Starlight Theatre. Interview by author. 22 December, 1989. Kansas City, Missouri.

Long, Larry. Former ensemble director at Starlight Theatre. Interview by author. 20 March 1990. Chicago, Illinois.

Loughead, Elaine (Mrs. Russell Geschwind). Former ensemble director at Starlight Theatre. Interview by author. 10 February 1990. Little Rock, Arkansas.

Madden, Katie (Mrs. George Scott). Former singing ensemble member at Starlight Theatre. Interview by author. 6 June 1990. Kansas City, Missouri.

Maier, Ray. Former soundman for Starlight Theatre. Interview by author. 23 February 1990. Sibley, Missouri.

McQueeny, Peter. Son of the former publicity manager for Starlight Theatre. Interview by author. 15 July 1989. Kansas City, Missouri.

Miller, David. Former head spotlight operator for Starlight Theatre. Interview by author. 12 July 1990. Kansas City, Missouri.

Miller, David Michael. Former head spotlight operator for Starlight Theatre. Interview by author. 12 July 1990. Kansas City, Missouri.

Miller, John. Present head spotlight operator for Starlight Theatre. Interview by author. 13 July 1990. Kansas City, Missouri.

Obermeyer, Burt. Master electrician at Starlight Theatre. Interview by author. 2 July 1990. Kansas City, Missouri.

Obermeyer, Marlene. Wife of Burt Obermeyer, master electrician at Starlight Theatre. Interview by author. 2 July 1990. Kansas City, Missouri.

Rolfe, Mary Beth (Tritt). Assistant to the general manager at Starlight Theatre. Interview by author. 7 March 1990. Starlight Theatre. Kansas City, Missouri.

Rolfe, Robert. Present general manager of Starlight Theatre. Interview by author. 12 July 1989 and 9 February 1990. Starlight Theatre. Kansas City, Missouri.

Ryan, Dean. Former musical director at Starlight Theatre. Interview by author. 4 August 1990. Kansas City, Missouri.

Sherry, Victoria. (Mrs. Roland Fiore). Former leading lady at Starlight Theatre. Interview by author. 4 June 1990. New Hope, Pennsylvania.

Shoemaker, James. Park planner for the city of Kansas City, Missouri. Interview by author. 30 June 1989. Kansas City, Missouri.

Short, Steve. Former dance ensemble member at Starlight Theatre. Interview by author. 25 April 1990. Overland Park, Kansas.

Symon, William Jr. Son of the former business manager at Starlight Theatre. Interview by author. 28 December 1989. Leawood, Kansas.

Symon, Mrs. William (Margaret Lish). Wife of the former business manager at Starlight Theatre. Interview by author. 25 June 1989. Kansas City, Missouri.

Williams, K. General manager of the Starlight Musicals. Interview by author. 13 June 1990. Indianapolis, Indiana.